Explaining Money & Banking

Explaining Money & Banking

Byron B. Carson and Robert E. Wright

Explaining Money & Banking

Cover design by Byron B. Carson

Interior design by Exeter Premedia Services Private Ltd., Chennai, India

First published in 2023 by
Business Expert Press, LLC
222 East 46th Street, New York, NY 10017
www.businessexpertpress.com

ISBN-13: 978-1-63742-467-4 (paperback)
ISBN-13: 978-1-63742-468-1 (e-book)

Business Expert Press Economics and Public Policy Collection

First edition: 2023

10 9 8 7 6 5 4 3 2 1

Description

Turn Crisis Into Cash.

Money matters got a lot scarier in 2020, and there is no end to the volatility in sight. Crisis means danger but also opportunity. To turn a profit during the next bust, or the next burst of inflation, individual investors and businesspeople must understand the economics of money, banking, and finance.

That's what this book provides, in concise and understandable prose, with pictures. Understand inflation and interest rates, stock prices, money and monetary policy, and the basics of information and macroeconomic theory in short order.

You might not beat the market after reading just this book, but if you learn its lessons, the market won't beat up your business or investment portfolio the next time the economy tanks due to pandemic, war, high taxes, or alien invasion.

Keywords

money; banking; cryptocurrency; financial instruments; financial regulation; macroeconomic theory; securities valuation models; public choice economics

Contents

Preface

Money, banking, and financial markets improve our quality of life. Financial systems and institutions facilitate commerce and allow us to do more of what we want to do. We can go to the grocery store with the expectation of buying sustenance; we can lend money to a banker for decades with the expectations of easy access, security, and a future reward; we can even buy financial products to minimize risk and grow our personal wealth. With such financial orderings, people can do wondrous things: they can live lives of relative luxury; they can coordinate large-scale production processes; and they can finance artistic, educational, public health, and environmental projects to benefit large portions of people.

At the same time, people use money to do seemingly bad and objectively evil things: money buys illegal drugs, it's used to commit violent crimes, and it finances warfare. People can do evil things without money too, but these are activities that might benefit some people without clearly improving well-being. The duality of money and finance is all the more reason to understand how these institutions work—so we might consider adjusting them to improve people's lives.

We have an optimistic view of money, banking, and financial markets that clashes with common thought we see in movies, social media, and in the news. When was the last time you heard someone extolling of the benefits of money, banks, and financial markets? Further, most people only think about money when they don't have the desired amount. And when markets don't work, like during crashes, recessions, and depressions, we are quick to criticize money, banks, commerce, and various *isms* usually involving capital. Google searches for the word *money*—shown in Figure P.1—increased during the Global Financial Crisis, often wrongly attributed to market failures, and the COVID-19 pandemic.

The economic way of thinking belies our optimism toward money and finance and the presentation throughout this book. This is an approach—a lens—to better understand how individuals make choices according to expected costs and benefits, how those choices influence

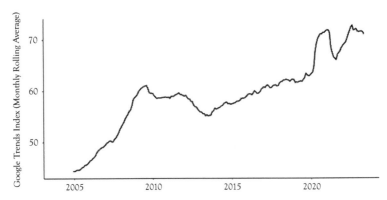

Figure P.1 Interest in money, 2004 to 2023

Source: Google Trends.

the decisions other people face, and how all of these choices intermingle to produce emergent, generally beneficial outcomes. There is much to be optimistic about in economics and finance, and we want to persuade you of this approach. To that end, we do our best to provide up-to-date evidence and scholarship demonstrating these ideas. Most of the figures clearly show changes in economic activity we think demonstrates an idea or an opportunity to ask interesting questions; we used R Studio and packages like fredr to gather data from FRED (Federal Reserve Economic Data) to make these graphs. We also highlight areas of disagreement—these debates are learning opportunities, not for the faint of heart or dogmatists. Economics is a lively, active discipline in part because of its openness for divergent assumptions and viewpoints.

More important than persuasion, perhaps, we want you to *internalize* the economic way of thinking as it relates to money, banking, and financial markets. Financial products are constantly evolving, new controversies arise, and novel financial crises are expected. With the ability to apply the economic insights learned in this book and from your professors, you can use the concepts discussed here to better understand the myriad changes in our financial system.

Regardless of what we might say or how people think of money, banking, and financial markets, commerce continues and economies grow. It is incumbent on us to better understand these topics and the role money and finance play. We will do this with plain language, with humor, and with clear graphics. Money and financial topics can be complex, but this is not an excuse for ignorance. You might have little desire to learn about these topics, you might think that derivatives are too complicated, and you might have friends and family who express disdain for these mundane issues. Unfortunately, this will not prevent the next Great Recession or Great Inflation, let alone lesser recessions and price movements, and they won't encourage central banks to enact appropriate monetary policy.

PART I

The Economics of Money

CHAPTER 1

The Role of Money and Banks in the World

Money Fulfils Individual Aspirations

People dream of doing wonderful things with their lives; they want to go to college; they want to care for pets and start families; they want to build businesses. These are the kinds of activities that give life meaning and allow people to flourish. Unfortunately, these goals do not just happen with a snap of the fingers. How is it that people buy simple goods and services, and how are transactions the hallmark of commercial interactions? How do people become college students when they are young, relatively inexperienced and unproductive, and with few assets? How is it that people pay for unexpected costs that arise when caring for pets and for loved ones? And how might entrepreneurs plan for long-term expenses? These are basic issues everyone faces when pursuing our respective plans—you, Robert and Byron, your neighbors, your college roommate, and even the relatively wealthy Wall Street financier.

How people respond to these problems—and use the knowledge of money, banking, and financial markets to overcome them—is an often overlooked factor of human flourishing. Consider the following situations.

We all know of Jack and the Beanstalk, how we should listen to mother, refrain from buying magical beans, or, rather, take advantage of unexpected opportunities. While we often focus on Jack's antics with the giant, we forget the exchange that took place earlier in the story, as well as the implications for the role money plays in everyday life.[1] The beans–cow exchange is simple enough: Jack wanted the beans to improve the lives of his family, and the seller wanted the cow.

---

[1] See Skwire (2014) for more on exchange in fairy tales.

The important point here is that the exchange made both sides better off. Jack's mother would disagree, and she expresses this disagreement throughout most of the story we've heard. What we often fail to recognize, however, is that Jack and his mother had different values or definitions of what makes for a better life. Jack wanted beans and his mother wanted money. Money for what? That is the interesting question we often gloss over, but it is a cornerstone of this text and the economic approach to money and banking.

Money is most importantly a means of exchange, and it helps people acquire other goods and services they value. All goods and services are goods, as opposed to bads, so we will often use the inclusive term goods to simplify. As such, money facilitates and clarifies most of our commercial interactions. Jack's mother probably wanted money to buy food or clothes. She knew that the grocer or the seamstress might not want a cow, but they probably would have taken money—so they could then buy goods they considered valuable. From this perspective, Jack and the Beanstalk is a tale encouraging the use of commonly accepted means of exchange, that is, don't take the weird beans, stick with money.

Here is another common scenario. Sam and Patrick are about to graduate from high school, and they are considering college. They expect college to provide them with a deeper appreciation for learning, hard skills for the job market, and increased lifetime earnings. Most of these benefits are probably likely. They also expect college to be expensive because, as shown in Figure 1.1, it is expensive, about eight times more expensive today than in 1980.

Sam worked throughout high school, and she has some savings. But she doesn't have near enough to pay for tuition even if she continues to work throughout college. Patrick has similar expectations about college, he didn't work throughout high school as he focused on his schoolwork. He earned some academic scholarships, but still doesn't have enough to pay full tuition.

Sam and Patrick face a remarkably common situation—like that of buying a car or a house—they want to purchase a good now, but they cannot pay the full amount today. If Sam is more financially aware and

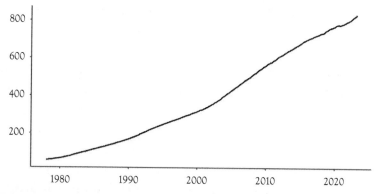

Figure 1.1 Consumer price index for tuition, school fees, and child care, 1978 to 2023

Source: FRED database using fredr.

acquires student loans, whereas Patrick does not, that could mean the difference between financing tuition over decades or all at once. And imagine if Sam knew more about what interest rates mean, that is, an opportunity cost, or the difference between fixed and variable rates. Patrick might acquire the same amount of student loans but with higher interest rates and higher costs. The higher cost of Patrick's loans might outweigh the benefit of the diploma. In any event, knowledge of these financial products, or the lack of knowledge, indicates people might have made different choices.

Consider Jamison, a 24-year-old bachelor rising through the ranks of a tech firm. Jamison just bought a dog—the cute, cuddly, floofy kind—to stay active and meet people. The puppy, which he names Princess, is adorable and a good girl. A couple months go by full of long walks, torn shoes, and much fun; however, Jamison's dog wakes up one day with the sniffles. He takes Princess to the vet, and they learn she has a serious case of pneumonia. He knows he can pay the bill over time, so he takes out a credit card specifically for Princess. Upon reflection, Jamison realizes he was lucky to have received credit, and that he might not be so lucky in the future—his job is uncertain, he might move, and he wants to start saving for retirement. To avoid the cost of these unexpected events, he searches for a way to smooth these expenses over time. He could save, but he worries about more severe events; what if Princess develops a tumor, or what if she is hit by a car? These are tragic events that his savings wouldn't be able to cover. Jamison keeps searching for a solution. What he *discovers* is a financial instrument people have been using for centuries, that is, insurance. He agrees to an insurance plan for Princess, for which he will pay a monthly fee, that is, a *premium*, in return for coverage of medical expenses if needed. Jamison now feels more secure in being able to cover future pet-related expenses and pursue his other goals.

Finally, financial institutions like banks and financial instruments like bonds, stocks, and derivatives provide individuals with expectations of future streams of income. Andrei is planning to expand his coffee shop business—made unique by his grandmother's special latte and biscuit recipes. He has built up some savings from the proceeds of the original shop but is still a long way away from what it would take to expand. He seeks out a loan from the bank, but he wants to provide them with additional reassurance. He contacts the local farmers he sources from and asks them to lock in prices today and exchange the goods later; such contracts are simply called forward contracts.

From these simplified scenarios, we can start to see how our lives are markedly improved from the advent of money, the development of financial intermediaries like banks and insurance companies, and the creation of financial instruments like forward contracts.

Financial Markets Are Complex but Not Complicated

Obviously, there is much more to money and banking than these simple stories. Buying groceries, taking on student loans, acquiring insurance, and expanding a local coffee shop are important parts of modern economic activity, but they are small parts of the myriad actions and interactions people take to pursue their goals. These general goals include consuming goods, saving and investing, increasing wealth, mitigating risk and uncertainty. Much of our financial system—densely interconnected networks of intermediaries that exchange capital, share risk, and facilitate the exchange of goods from place-to-place and across time—facilitates these goals.

There are thousands of banks in the United States, for example, that serve millions of people with goods ranging from offering checking and savings accounts to making loans. Figure 1.2 shows the number of commercial banks in the United States. You might notice that the number of banks is declining; while there were over 14,000 banks in 1985, there are over 4,000 banks in 2020. Despite this decline and for reasons we will discuss later, the banks that remain are larger on average.

People write insurance contracts to mitigate the cost of many kinds of risk. We often think of health insurance and car insurance—those insurance contracts are very important parts of our lives—but we might also acquire insurance for unemployment, pet care, for flooding, for asteroid damage, for future coronavirus epidemics, and so on, and for losses that will occur but without being able to know when or to whom. Figure 1.3 shows the rate of auto insurance claims across multiple categories has been consistent for the last two decades, which speaks to the persistent desire for auto insurance.

And consider stocks and the markets where stocks are bought and sold. Such markets are another way to acquire external finance, especially when the cost of borrowing might otherwise be expensive. Figure 1.4 shows the growth of the Wilshire 5000—an index of the stock prices for most of the stocks traded in the United States—which indicates the growing importance of stock markets in financial systems.

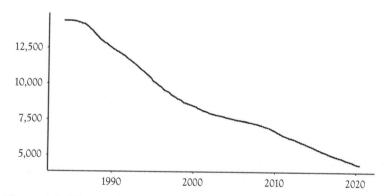

Figure 1.2 The number of commercial banks in the United States, 1984 to 2020

Source: FRED database using fredr.

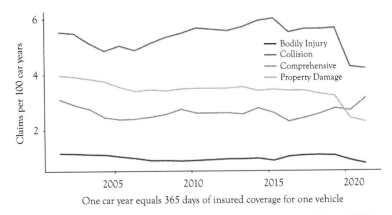

One car year equals 365 days of insured coverage for one vehicle

Figure 1.3 *Private passenger auto insurance claims, 2001 to 2020*

Source: Insurance Information Institute.

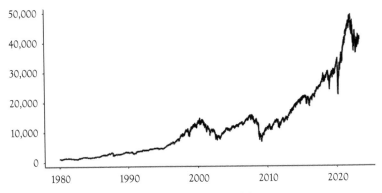

Figure 1.4 *The Wilshire 5000, 1980 to 2023*

Source: FRED database using fredr.

These interactions suggest that financial systems are not complicated, but they are *complex*. They are the result of human actions and interactions, not of human design. Think of Play-Doh—the more you add, the more the structure can change and morph into a structure much different from its constituent parts. The analogy to financial markets suggests that there are myriad opportunities to use money, to save, and to invest. Similarly, there are many opportunities to develop a comparative advantage in some aspect of financial markets. Some banks are better suited to offer loans to farmers, others are better at lending to real estate developers. As financial intermediaries develop their own comparative advantage, the division of labor expands, and the gains from exchange become larger, which extends to banks and their acquisition of different specialties. These intermediaries and the complex market within which they operate will tend to attract more customers, facilitate more plans, and make people better off.

This means there is much complexity inherent in larger commercial societies because of these interactions and because of the myriad financial arrangements people make to facilitate those interactions. Such complexity is a blessing and a curse. We have many opportunities to save, invest, and mitigate risk, which all improve welfare. Much of modern human flourishing can be attributed to the development of financial systems. Just as important, financial systems provide people with opportunities to acquire *external finance* or funds that do not come from savings or a wealthy relative. The next time you seek a car loan or renew your student loans, consider how your life might be without a financial system in place. Figure 1.5 shows over time the size of America's financial sector compared to the size of its economy. The trend is generally upward, a phenomenon some call financialization, which refers to a growing, more interconnected financial system.

But the interconnections between money, financial markets, and many other markets suggests that when money and price signals denominated in money become distorted, general economic activity becomes distorted too. Such distortions lead to periods of boom and bust, recessions, or

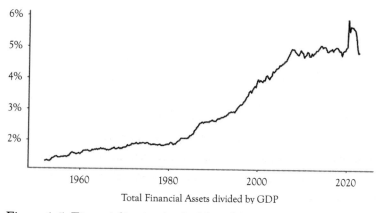

Total Financial Assets divided by GDP

Figure 1.5 Financialization in the United States, 1952 to 2022

Source: FRED database using fredr.

depressions. These are periods where the owners and managers of a firm realize they have to let people go; these are periods where people perceive little hope and rates of suicide rise; these are periods where people can lose significant portions of their wealth.

Aside from financial crises, individuals and financial intermediaries face a pretty onerous problem—one of the most severe problems in financial markets—information asymmetry. That is, whenever one party to an exchange has more information about a transaction than another, information asymmetry problems ensue. Like a hydra, there are multiple kinds of information asymmetry problems: adverse selection arises before a contract is signed, whereas moral hazard problems arise after a contract is signed. These problems raise Cain for market participants as they can make negotiations nigh impossible and can encourage duplicitous behavior, both of which distort financial markets.

Information asymmetry problems are some of the thorniest, ever present problems people face in financial markets. As we will soon show, however, financial intermediaries and financial systems seek to resolve these problems. For example, banks develop a comparative advantage in pooling information about loan applicants, which they can use to better assess the quality of borrowers, or the likelihood of repayment. Such an ability makes them more likely to lend and facilitate acquisition of external finance. Problems of asymmetric information never go away, but banks and other financial intermediaries can attenuate them.

We can better appreciate these complexities, problems related to information asymmetries and others, learn how to better consider investment opportunities, and improve financial systems with the help of the economic way of thinking.

Money and Finance Seems Old Hat

Money, banking, and financial markets might seem like boring topics or issues beyond anyone's control. They become fascinating, however, when viewed from the perspective of the economic way of thinking. Consider the variety of financial instruments—legal contracts that oblige one party to provide payment or otherwise entail some kind of property right. The language of contract and property rights is particularly helpful as it clarifies the kind of behaviors and relationships people must exhibit when they use financial instruments. There are three broad kinds of these instruments: debt, equity, and hybrid. Debt instruments, like bonds, indicate a lender–borrower relationship in which the borrower promises to pay a fixed sum and interest to the lender at a specific date or over some period. Equity instruments, like stocks, are similar to debt instruments, but they entail ownership rights and rights to some portion of a firm's profit. Hybrid instruments, like preferred stock, are a combination of debt and equity instruments; for example, a preferred stock promises a fixed payment but only on the condition that a company earns sufficient profit.

We can now add a bit more realism to our financial system; we have money, financial intermediaries, and financial instruments. We have most of the ingredients that make for a developing financial system.

The Grammar of Finance and the Economic Way of Thinking Colors Our World

Financial systems are some of the oldest institutions people have. Money—in the sense of a widespread means of exchange—emerges from exchange, and people have been exchanging goods for untold millennia. As we will learn in the next chapter, money also facilitates exchange. Once people have accepted a common means of exchange, for example, they can spend less time negotiating over the value of goods. For all the differences people might have, money facilitates exchange. People might hate each other, they might want to go to war with others, but money provides a way to facilitate peaceful interactions. We can live our lives in better ways because money facilitates exchange—from one place to another and across time.

Considering all of the possible interactions money and financial instruments afford, we need a way to organize our thoughts and better understand how individuals behave and interact with each other. This is exactly why economics—and the economic way of thinking—is so useful. The lens it provides gives us insight into why people behave in particular ways. Here's the short version: people do more of things that are beneficial and less of things that are costly. That is, people do more of something until the marginal or additional costs outweigh the marginal benefits. This logic is utterly simple, but its implications run deep and offer much explanatory power. We will be sure to highlight these implications as we go forward.

We can highlight one of these implications if we revisit Sam in her search for a student loan. Her decision to accept a loan offer depends on the marginal benefit of paying tuition today and the marginal cost of the interest rate—the opportunity cost of taking the loan.[2] Imagine if Sam is willing to take out a $30,000 loan with an interest rate of 5 percent. She can take the money now and pay for her next year of school, but when she has to repay the loan, she will have to repay the $30,000 plus the interest. She might be willing to take the loan as the interest rate rises to 7 percent, but definitely not if it goes to 10 percent. To her, the marginal cost is too high at a rate of 10 percent; she would rather use her money to open up a coffee shop. This is marginal thinking at work.

Together, They Illuminate Our History

The economic analysis of money and banking—marginal thinking in a world of scarce resources—also makes us better observers of past events. The more you know how money operates to facilitate exchange, how banks facilitate interactions between borrowers and lenders, how stock markets work, and so on, the more you can understand the peculiarities of history. There are many examples, but let's look at examples from England, the United States, and France before the turn of the 18th century.

The rise of modern banking in London followed goldsmiths—craftsmen who developed a comparative advantage in assessing the value of gold, in storing and securing it, and in exchanging it. These banking intermediaries became a primary source of credit in 17th-century London, especially after Charles I seized the mint where many had previously held their liquid assets.

---

[2] This kind of cost recognizes that choices entail foregone opportunities, that is, opportunities that are lost because a choice was made. In this way, we are really concerned with the marginal opportunity cost: all costs are opportunity costs, and all costs are marginal costs.

In the United States, in urban areas like Philadelphia and New York, financial markets developed in the late 18th century in street markets and coffee houses (see, for example, Wright 2005). These opportunities to buy and sell securities and bonds encouraged vibrant financial markets, which encouraged widespread economic activity.

As for France, we can better understand some of the repercussions of the French Assembly's actions that precipitated the revolts of the late 1780s and the oncoming revolution. For instance, a moderate inflationary period followed the Assembly's confiscation of Church lands in the late 1780s, which the Assembly used to pay pre-existing debts. In their efforts to encourage the use of assignats as currency, the Convention also *required* their acceptance at par value in June 1793; the Convention had fully repudiated the first issue of assignats by July 1793. Such policies led to an inflation rate of more than 11,000 percent between 1794 and 1796 (Cutsinger, Ingber, and Rouanet 2020). It is reasonable to suggest then that the inflationary period of the early 1790s—and the hyperinflation just a few years later—contributed to the distortions of commerce and economic calculation, as well as additional discontent and revolt (Sargent and Velde 1995).

Elevate Public Discourse

Much of our common discourse is confused on issues relating to money and banking. For example, Bernie Sanders ran part of his presidential campaign on a platform to cap interest rates for all consumer loans and credit cards at 15 percent. Never mind that John Locke—writing in the late 1600s—explained why such a policy does more harm than good. Locke argued that a cap would create a shortage of loanable funds as there would be too many borrowers relative to lenders. Such a policy might then benefit rich people and harm poor people. Read your Locke, Bernie!

Recently, many people in the United States became transfixed as the stock prices of Gamestop and other companies—which were thought to be well along the road to bankruptcy—went up and down. Carson had several students who voiced criticism of these firms, along with the app they had used to buy and sell shares. They were concerned about their investments, and they were concerned about what such events meant for

American society. Does Robinhood provide access to markets, or is it yet another way capitalism sticks it to the little guy?

And, Make Us Wealthier

Understanding economics might make you wealthier, but be warned that few economists own their own island. James Buchanan—quoting Frank Ward—puts it this way, "The study of economics won't keep you out of the breadline; but at least you'll know why you're there."

Joking aside, we contend that the clarity provided through the economic way of thinking can make you wealthier than you might have been otherwise. This is likely as you learn more about how financial instruments and markets work, as well as the various ways central banks influence monetary policy. The insights explored next can also help shed light on which investments are more or less profitable.

More importantly, a better understanding of these financial matters makes us all better off. The more others develop an appreciation for financial markets and the institutions that foster such things, the more extensive they might become. That stands to make a larger portion of people—throughout the world—better off.

CHAPTER 2

Money

Money and Sand in the Gears of Commerce

Money is, perhaps, the most important invention no one person invented. There are two important claims we should unpack. First, we posit that money is an incredible innovation—an innovation that is potentially the most important. It unclogs the fountains of commerce—to extend Adam Smith's phraseology of 1776 when *An Inquiry into the Nature and Causes of the Wealth of Nations* was published—and it offers *a way out*—to use Menger's description from his 1871 textbook *Principles of Economics*—of the crippling problem posed by barter. That is, by reducing the transaction costs of most of the exchanges people want to make, the things we—and other people in society—call money are so helpful because they economize on time. Instead of searching for a person who wants to accept the chickens I have for what they are willing to sell, we can use money. Instead of haggling over the value of my chickens—they are prize worthy chickens—where few are willing to pay what I think they are worth, we can use money.

Money is more important than cars and airplanes and, perhaps, our beloved Internet and smartphones. We wouldn't have such things if people had to barter rather than use money. By lowering transaction costs and encouraging mutually beneficial exchange, money increases the well-being of the individuals making the exchange, and it increases wealth. In a technical sense, we mean that the use of money—as a means of exchange—increases consumer and producer surplus. These are, respectively, differences between (1) what a consumer is willing to pay and what they actually pay for a good and (2) what a producer receives and what they would have taken for a good. Just as the wheel, electricity, and filtered water allow people to be more productive and live longer and happier lives—so does money.

Moreover, money facilitates economic calculation, a vital way in which people efficiently allocate scarce resources. Imagine you want to produce a chair, which you can make out of gold, platinum, wood, plastic, or many other inputs. There are many ways to make a chair, but only some of the inputs will make a chair that satisfies the desires of both the producer and consumers. Without some guide, you might not know which input satisfies those desires. Money prices that accurately convey relative scarcity—derived in a competitive market where property rights are protected—provide such a guide (Mises 1922). Golden chairs are probably too expensive, given their opportunity cost, and few people might want to pay for them. Wooden chairs, however, seem more appropriate. Money prices provide a rich source of knowledge to buyers and sellers about underlying market conditions (Hayek 1945).

The second claim suggests that no one person created money. This includes the smartest people living today, cave dwelling *Homo sapiens*, and everyone in between. Think about it! Where did you get the money you have in your wallet—if you still carry cash? You might have received it from a bank, but where did they receive it from? You might suggest a government issued those notes. That might be true, but why did that government decide to issue those notes? They have a comparative advantage in the use of force, and they could have commanded the use of any currency.

Money emerges from the actions and interactions of individuals choosing different goods based on the expected costs and benefits to themselves. As people become more productive and they demand a larger quantity and variety of goods, barter becomes imminently difficult. To lower those costs—to eliminate the double coincidence of wants—individuals realize the value in holding goods other people might want even if they themselves do not. Menger suggests that money emerges from our concern for ourselves *and* from our concern for others. He states, "Possession of these commodities [i.e., money] would considerably facilitate his search for persons who have just the goods he needs" (Menger 2007, 259). By being considerate of what others want, you are better able to improve your own welfare.

For those reasons, money takes the cake despite how it is often characterized inappropriately. We often think of it as income—a claim on resources expressed in money terms—but the more important characteristic of money is that it serves as a means of exchange. It can also be a unit of account and a store of value. Each is an important feature of how we commonly use money.

Thus, money does not simply refer to the physical notes we spend at the grocery store, that circulate through a financial system, and that governments issue. Money refers to the expectations people have for *transferability*—their ability to use money in future exchange. If people expected only a handful of people might want the type of money they have to offer, or that they could not easily transfer it, they'd soon find something else to use as money.

Better to Have Had Money and Lost It Than to Have Never Had Money at All

If you are still unsure about this, consider what happens when people cannot use money. Consider people with barter economies, people with inflating or depreciating currencies, and people where money is prohibited.

Every modern society makes the transition from barter to money, but not every society has made such advances. Outside of families and small-scale communities—wherein groups do not require the use of money to allocate resources—people quickly adopt money to exchange. Money lowers the transaction costs associated with exchange and facilitates economic calculation.

Further, people might have money, but its value as a means of exchange becomes distorted with inflation—a decline in the value of money that leads to a higher price level. The rate of inflation might become so high that people stop using money altogether. This means people stop using money prices, and they are less able to plan and economize on scarce resources.

We often hear about historical periods of inflation and hyperinflation, for example, Weimar Germany, but it remains a problem even today. Consider Venezuela after 2012, where official government estimates of the annual rate of inflation—shown in Figure 2.1—show a significant rise in inflation.

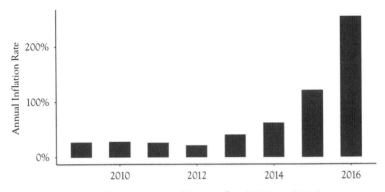

Figure 2.1 *The inflation rate in Venezuela, 2009 to 2016*

Source: FRED database using fredr.

Steve Hanke—in the Hanke Inflation Dashboard—uses high-frequency, free-market exchange rate data along with the theory of purchasing power parity to construct another measure of inflation (Hanke 2021). Hanke suggests that exchange rates change with inflation rates—topics we explore in Chapter 8. Hanke also uses a larger basket of goods to reflect how widespread changes in inflation actually are. Figure 2.2 shows the annualized rate of inflation using Hanke's approach for Venezuela between 2017 and 2020, which suggests that Venezuela recently experienced one of the worst episodes of hyperinflation in human history (Hanke and Bushnell 2017).

Such high rates of inflation mean that people cannot use the Venezuelan Bolivar like they did in the past. That is, its value as a means of exchange has eroded; people cannot use it to buy things they want. People are more likely to use Bolivars to weave into a bag.

There are more pernicious effects of rising rates of inflation, and to say that the quality of life has fallen is an understatement. As the value of the Venezuelan Bolivar became inflated, that is, worth less, people use it less. This transition leaves people bartering and in an ongoing scramble to find vendors willing to sell goods they want *and* to accept goods they have. Remember barter exposes one to a significant amount of transaction costs, costs that money eliminates.

As such, food and medicine shortages are rampant, as are crime and migration rates. Shortages arise as higher rates of inflation create an intertemporal coordination problem. As the value of currency falls, retailers are

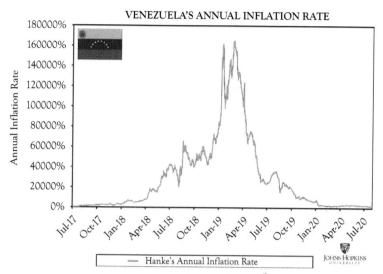

Figure 2.2 *Inflation in Venezuela according to Hanke, 2017 to 2020*

Sources: U.S Bureau of Labor Statistics, AirTM
Calculations by Prof. Steve H. Hanke, The Johns Hopkins University.
Note: These inflation rates are implied by the movements in the black-market VES/USD exchange rate; values under 25% should be considered unreliable.

less likely to stock their shelves and customers are more likely to buy physical goods. Crime rates might rise as people realize they can acquire what they want by force rather than a peaceful, mutually beneficial exchange. "Empty stomachs are driving people from all walks of life into crime," *Time* writer Ciara Nugent notes, "and fueling an unprecedented wave of violence that claims 73 lives each day" (Nugent 2018). People also begin to realize that leaving the country might be a way to attenuate these problems. Indeed, the UN Refugee Agency estimates that the number of Venezuelans seeking refugee status has increased by 8,000 percent since 2014.

Grocery stores and *bodegons* that imported goods and accepted other currencies—typically U.S. dollars (USD) and sometimes cryptocurrencies—stand in stark contrast to the surrounding misery in Venezuela. Such stores are relatively well-stocked and reliable sources of goods. Such outcomes are related to the value of currency. As people have relatively good expectations about the value of alternative currencies, like USD, they are willing to use them in exchange if they can acquire them. Inflation is not the only cause of human suffering, but it is among the most controllable.

Not Interested in Money? Look Around You

This perspective on money becomes a critique of common notions of money as a source of greed or as a tool of capitalism. Once we consider money as a medium of exchange—an institution that is an ever-present part of human society—arguments against it become much more difficult to make. You might not like money, or you might think it debases human nature, but that does not mean other people should be prevented from bettering themselves. The more you advocate that we should not use money, the more you are arguing to raise transaction costs on others and to distort their ability to engage in economic calculation.

When people can use money and maintain its value, they tend to become more prosperous. This is why the Economic Freedom of the World project, produced by the Fraser Institute, includes measures of stable money in its index (Gwartney et al. 2021). Societies that have more stable monetary regimes also tend to have higher levels of economic freedom. Table 2.1, for example, lists the countries with the lowest and highest values of access to sound money.

From POW Camps to Prisons

Our thoughts on money are not new, but we argue they are conditional—again something few recognize. That is, the use of money depends on the

Table 2.1 Access to sound money, 2021

Country	Sound Money Score	Country	Sound Money Score
Jordan	9.87	Papua New Guinea	6.04
Albania	9.86	Syrian Arab Republic	5.98
Panama	9.86	Congo, Dem. Rep.	5.68
Switzerland	9.85	Ukraine	5.61
New Zealand	9.78	Congo, Rep.	5.14
Cabo Verde	9.77	Angola	4.93
Costa Rica	9.77	Argentina	4.00
Montenegro	9.77	Zimbabwe	3.41
Israel	9.76	Sudan	1.82
Singapore	9.76	Venezuela, RB	.69

expectations people have over its future use. There is not a better way to examine some of these conditions than to analyze cases where people are placed in extreme situations, that is, situations where we might think money shouldn't work. R. A. Radford wrote a famous study on money in a prisoner of war (POW) camp during the Second World War (Radford 1945); he became an expert on the subject from personal experience as a POW.

POW camps are interesting for our conversations related to money because POWs might speak different languages, and they have few of the freedoms people have in normal commercial settings. The central problem is an economic one. That is, given somewhat regular aid disbursements from the Red Cross and whatever else POWs could scrounge up, prisoners often found they did not have what they wanted. They might have received too many chocolate bars, or they might have found they wanted more cigarettes. Seemingly, they were stuck; they might not have been able to bribe a guard, let alone go to the grocery store. Yet, they developed money to resolve their problems.

While the POWs didn't have an explicit currency they could use as money, they used the next best thing given their circumstances, namely cigarettes. As people spent more time in the POW camp, they realized cigarettes became something everyone valued; it became a good people either wanted to have and smoke, or it became something they could use to exchange for other goods. Radford utilizes much of the insights we have about money in his analysis.

Even in prisons—another instance where people are not allowed to engage in normal commercial activity—people find ways to use money. Instead of physical currency, they also use cigarettes. And if they cannot use cigarettes—because they were outlawed in all federal prisons for health reasons—they find substitutes, like precooked ramen noodles (Collins and Alvarez 2015).

Measurement and Meaning in Money

Given the myriad kinds of money people have used, it will become useful to categorize and focus on measuring the amount of money in circulation. For most commercial societies, this means measuring the amount of relatively saleable or liquid kinds of money, for example, cash, checkable deposits, savings, travelers checks, and so on. Imagine a spectrum of liquidity with cash on one end—the relatively liquid end—and thinly traded bonds on the other end. That is basically how most scholars and officials measure money. They just call it M1, M2, M3, and so on. Figure 2.3 shows how two of the most common measures of money, M1 and M2, have changed since 1959.

Figure 2.3 shows that there were over 20,000 billion (20 trillion) dollars in circulation for M1—as of April 2022. According to the Federal Reserve, the M1 measure includes the following:

1. Currency outside the U.S. Treasury, Federal Reserve Banks, and the vaults of depository institutions.
2. Demand deposits at commercial banks (excluding those amounts held by depository institutions, the U.S. government, and foreign banks and official institutions) less cash items in the process of collection and Federal Reserve float.
3. Other liquid deposits, consisting of other checkable deposits (OCDs) and savings deposits (including money market deposit accounts). Seasonally adjusted M1 is constructed by summing currency, demand deposits, and OCDs (before May 2020) or other liquid deposits (beginning May 2020), each seasonally adjusted separately.

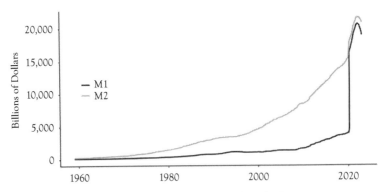

Figure 2.3 M1 and M2 money supply, 1959 to 2023

Source: FRED database using fredr.

M2 includes:

1. M1
2. Savings deposits (including money market deposit accounts)
3. Small-denomination time deposits (time deposits in amounts of less than $100,000), less individual retirement account (IRA), and Keogh balances at depository institutions
4. Balances in retail money market funds (MMFs) less IRA and Keogh balances at MMFs

The form money takes—and how it is measured—evolves depending on the goals people have and their incentives to exchange. Bitcoin and other cryptocurrencies, private accounting entries with no physical existence, are no different. Recent development and innovation regarding cryptocurrencies and blockchain technology follow the goals people have regarding long distance exchange, anonymity, a hedge against inflation, and so on. (For more on the economics and institutions of blockchain, see Berg, Davidson, and Potts 2020.) Cryptocurrencies like Bitcoin might not seem like money to most, but it does serve as a limited medium of exchange (Hazlett and Luther 2020). We should expect ownership of cryptocurrencies to grow, and we should also expect the emergence of even newer kinds of money.

PART II

The Economics of Time, Risk, and Uncertainty

CHAPTER 3

Time Preference

You probably won't ever hear noneconomists speak of *time preference,* but you do hear people talk about interest rates; they are intimately related. Time preference refers to a person's willingness to consume goods now or later, and we often rely on interest rates to indicate or measure time preference. This preference explains how people address tradeoffs associated with the passage of time. It also provides a simple way to evaluate a variety of financial assets and entrepreneurial projects. So, if you want to choose between different time-dependent investment opportunities, understanding interest can help you make better, more profitable decisions.

Do you like having some stuff now rather than lots of stuff later? Or maybe you prefer to delay a little bit of consumption today in exchange for more consumption tomorrow? Regardless of your answer to those questions, your answer depends on your time preference. Furthermore, we should recognize that people have a positive rate of time preference, given they are not willing to forego all present consumption. People have to eat today if they want to live tomorrow.

Here is another way to consider time preference. Imagine your favorite social media influencer tells you the world is ending in 24 hours and you believe the message. What would you do? What would other people do? We should expect that with so little time, people would prefer consumption today rather than tomorrow. Indeed, whatever people might consume or whatever plans they might make after tomorrow would become much less valuable. This is a situation where your time preference has become very high and you prefer immediate rather than delayed satisfaction.

Spot Transactions Are Nice, But Intertemporal Transactions Are Nicer

To develop our intuition about time preference and interest, first think about *spot* transactions. Many of the day-to-day transactions we make, for example, like paying for groceries *on the spot*, are spot or immediate exchanges. Spot transactions reduce the chance for fraud as both parties have a fairly good idea of what is being exchanged. Also, the goods and money are exchanged simultaneously. The downside of spot transactions is that goods received must be consumed soon thereafter. That is, you wouldn't buy on the spot market today a box of cereal to eat in one year; that would be some stale cereal. But you might contract today to buy that cereal in a year in what is called the forward market.

Many people—for many centuries—have realized they might want to acquire goods today and pay later. Or they might provide goods today and accept payment later. Both are examples of what is termed the credit market.

Credit markets have nothing to do with being lazy, a cheat, or poor. Or a greedy lender. Intertemporal exchanges are common, valuable components of economic activity, and make both parties to an exchange better off. Think about cases where you have paid for a good for which the benefits of that good accrue later, for example, the roofing of a house might take a couple days to install, but it provides shelter for years, student debtors receive education over the short term and pay the loan over a longer period, and homeowners buy a house and pay a *mortgage*. These are intertemporal exchanges.

These kinds of exchanges make for distinct problems because time is now a factor; time raises the potential for a different kind of opportunity cost as well as risk. The opportunity cost of lending, for example, refers to the forsaken value of opportunities that could have been pursued over the period of the loan. Similarly, the risk of appropriation becomes more important as time separates the point at which a person receives a good and the point at which a person pays (or is paid).

Credit is often maligned, but it is a way to finance unexpected expenses. If you don't have enough in savings, if you incur unexpected medical expenses, or if you want to take a trip to Bali, credit can help. Someone, somewhere out there in the wide financial world, is willing to finance those expenses for you; in return, they expect you will pay them back. You can pay for that surgery you wanted or go to Bali when you want.

People have used credit and related insurance contracts to facilitate long-term plans for centuries. In the United States at least, credit is an important source of external finance for individuals and businesses (Durkin et al. 2014). Long before we could get loans via our smartphones, we accessed credit through country stores and local banks.

We've come a long way since the country store days of credit. Figure 3.1, for example, shows the total dollar amount of bank loans and leases and an upward trend. People can now find credit at megabanks that span continents, credit card issuers, and specialized finance companies.

Credit influences production, not just consumption. When entrepreneurs want to advance their businesses or open new shops or other facilities, acquiring goods now and paying for them later might be appropriate, rational, and profitable.

These intertemporal transactions expand the goods people can acquire. How neat! They mean people can acquire goods now and pay later. Despite what late-night commentators might decry, rarely are credit recipients taken advantage of; both sides of such exchanges expect to be made better off. Indeed, the lion's share of credit is paid back.

How does this kind of market come about, and how do individual borrowers match with lenders? We will explicitly answer this question

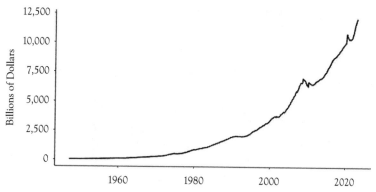

Figure 3.1 Bank loans and leases, 1947 to 2023

Source: FRED database using fredr.

soon, but first, we suggest that it happens like any other market—through the price system. Prices are knowledge surrogates. That is, they coordinate the actions of myriad individuals—and their values and preferences—to economize on goods that have become relatively scarce and encourage the consumption of goods that are relatively abundant. Prices coordinate most markets, including credit markets, by linking disparate buyers (borrowers) and sellers (lenders). In credit markets, the rate of interest is the primary price that acts as the coordinating device.

Importantly, the rate of interest is the opportunity cost of lending funds. It simultaneously represents the value a lender must give up to lend and the value a borrower will give up to repay the loan. Instead of lending you $5,000 at an interest rate of 5 percent, say for a trip to Bali—so you can have a nice time on the beach and down nice bottles of chilled rum—a lender could have lent those funds to someone who wants a car and was willing to pay 5 percent. Alternatively, the lender could have taken the trip to Bali. To receive the funds for the trip to Bali, borrowers must pay the lender's opportunity cost.

Not surprisingly, borrowers face this same logic. There is an opportunity cost to repaying the loan. If your $5,000 loan is to be repaid in equal installments over two years, for example, you would have to pay somewhere around $220 a month. The $220 you use to repay the loan and interest will not be available for you to purchase goods. Thus, the opportunity cost of repaying the loan is the value of what you would have purchased with the $220 every month. Imagine if the lender faced a higher opportunity cost and charged an interest rate of 20 percent. That means you have to pay back the *principal* plus interest of 20 percent and make monthly payments of over $250. Higher and higher opportunity costs might encourage you to pass on the loan and the trip to Bali altogether. In any event, interest rates coordinate the plans of lenders and borrowers.

The preceding logic is central to thinking about the economics of time and much of our discussion on monetary policy going forward. To refine this idea, we want to think about the following problems:

1. Is $1 worth more today or in one year?
2. How much will $500 today be worth in 100 years?

3. How much should you pay today for a government-issued bond with a face value of $1,000 that will mature in 30 years?

4. How much would it cost to endow a chair in honor of your favorite professor?

Each of these questions is best answered by thinking about the difference between *present* and *future* sums. This distinction—and thinking through some logical implications—does a lot of analytic work for the economic way of thinking. Let's walk through these questions.

We Can Anticipate How a Present Sum Grows

Most of us would respond to the first question by saying they would rather have $1 today. That is, $1 *today* > $1 *in* 1 *year*. Over the next year, you might have many opportunities to spend that $1; you would be worse off if you didn't have it until the end of the year. That intuition is exactly right, and it follows from our understanding of opportunity cost. Instead of taking the $1 in one year, you could have spent it and reaped the benefit or you could have lent it. If you are to forego the value of that $1, you need compensation. The logical relationship between present and future values follows this intuition.

If you are willing to accept $1 in one year with no other considerations, you ignore the opportunity cost of $1. It means you are willing to forego all consumption today in favor of consuming in the future. If you think about this long enough, you might realize that a person with this preference would start to get hungry after a couple days and eventually die. This is a good reason why economists often consider interest rates—as a measure of time preference—to be positive!

So, people prefer $1 in one year only when interest rates are sufficient to compensate them for the opportunity cost of lending.

We can now move on to the other questions, as we just established a simple (but not simplistic) way to consider the relationship between present and future values. Before we answer, however, we need to know a crucial piece of information. We need to specify a particular rate of interest. Let's say the prevailing market rate of interest is 5 percent. With such information provided, we can now understand how a present sum should be expected to grow.

Generally, a future value equals the sum of a present value and interest payments on the present value. So, if we had $500 today and the interest rate was 5 percent, its value in one year becomes: $500 + $500($i$) = $500(1 + i). Given our interest rate of 5 percent, we see that $500 becomes $525. We haven't answered our initial question yet, but it is a pretty neat result. We had $500 today, but it grew to $525 over one year.

You might think that if this sum acquired an additional $25—5 percent of $500 is $25—in one year, it would do so the next year, and the next year, and the next year, and so on. Indeed, each year is the same time period, and the rate of interest does not change, so it seems plausible that you can just add those interest payments up and add to the principal. If this is true, we should expect the initial $500 to become $3,000 in 100 years. This is logical, but only if the interest payments do not themselves accumulate interest. In many credit contracts, interest *compounds* over time, and the difference between it and simple (no-compounding) interest is large, especially over longer periods of time.

To see the additional value of compounding, consider how $500 grows over a period of two years. We have to consider the sum of the principal, the interest payment on the principal over the first year, the interest payment on the principal over the second year, *and* the interest payment on the interest payment over the first year: $PV + PV(i) + PV(i) + PV(i)(i) = PV(1 + 2i + i^2)$. Thus, $500 today becomes $500(1 + 2(.05) + .05^2) = 551.25 over two years. The interest on interest is the part we might easily forget. Including the interest on interest factor amounts to additional pennies in this case, but it adds up over time, especially at higher rates of interest. So, we want to consider the interest on interest on interest on interest, and so on.

Following the same pattern and logic for the third, fourth, fifth, tenth, and nth years, we can arrive at the correct answer. As you might expect, however, that process becomes cumbersome very quickly. Fortunately, that entire process simplifies to the following general formula describing the relationship between present and future values. Where present value is PV, future value is FV, the rate of interest is i, and the number of compounding periods is t, the formal relationship becomes: $FV = PV * (1 + i)^t$.

Thus, $500 today with a 5 percent interest rate becomes $65,750.62 over 100 years. That is an order of magnitude different from the mere $3,000 under a simple interest (no compounding) contract.

We Can Evaluate Future Streams of Income

Before we answer the third question, here is a simpler version. How much do you value $100 in two years at an interest rate of 5 percent? All we need to do here is recognize this problem as the reverse of the future value equation shown earlier. That is, we can rewrite our present and future value equation: $PV = \dfrac{FV}{(1+i)^t}$. Making the appropriate substitutions, we find that $90.70 approximates the value of $100 in two years if the appropriate rate of interest is 5 percent.

Now, consider the third question: it is the same question, just posed in a slightly different way—namely, with the use of a financial instrument called *bonds*. Bonds are a promise to pay the owner of the bond the face value upon the date of maturation. Discount bonds make a single payment at maturation, while coupon bonds promise periodic interest payments in addition to the principal sum at maturation.

A 30-year discount bond with a face value of $1,000—which means that in 30 years, you expect to receive a $1,000 payout—might be a good deal, at the right price that is. You wouldn't pay $1,000, given that we know you would want to be compensated. Maybe $800? Thirty years is a long time; maybe $500?

Substituting the given values for FV, i, and t, we see that the current price of this bond equals $231.37. Any price above that and you should reconsider acquiring the bond, that is, its purchase would not be worth the opportunity cost at an interest rate of 5 percent. Any price below that and you come out ahead!

This Logic Applies to Gifts From Grandmother

Here's an interesting extension. Imagine your grandmother hands you a birthday card and, next to the well wishes, she offers you the following deal. She offers to give you $500 today on the spot or the following payouts over the next 10 years: $1 in one year; $2 in two years; $4 in three years; $8 in four years; $16 in five years; $32 in six years; $64 in seven years; $128 in eight years; $256 in nine years; and $512 in 10 years. What should you do if we assume a constant rate of interest of 5 percent?

This question is not complicated; it merely asks you to add the present values of each of the payouts. That is, add the present value of $1 in one year, the present value of $2 in two years, the present value of $4 in three years, and so on. If you are willing to go through that process, you will find that the second option is actually more valuable because its present value is $660.68. Your grandmother is teaching you a valuable lesson about interest and valuing future streams of income. (And if she dies before 10 years and does not leave the stipulated sums to you in her will, she'll teach you lessons about the importance of life insurance and risk.) Thanks, grandma!

There Is Even Something for the Entrepreneur

You might have to choose between long-term projects with similar costs and benefits. It might not be immediately clear, however, which project maximizes net revenue. Some projects are clear enough. You should take the earlier payout, for example, if the choice is between a net revenue of $x today or anything less than $x in the future. And you can probably guess that a payout of $1,300 in two years is larger than the sum of a payout of $300 in one year and a payout of $900 in two years. Double check to make sure you understand why (assume an interest rate of 5 percent).

Comparing Multiple Projects

In other contexts, however, it might not be easy to intuit an answer. The following example clarifies such a problem and uses the relationship between present and future sums to provide additional confidence.

Project A costs $1,000 today but yields a payout of $1,700 in two years. Project B also costs $1,000 today but yields a payout of $500 in one year and $1,200 in two years. So the question becomes: if you only have $1,000 to spend today, which project has a higher net present value? Assume an interest rate of 5 percent.

To answer, we need to find the present values of each of the projects. Project A has a net present value of $1,541.95 – $1,000 = $541.95. Again, note that it is difficult to answer this question with certainty without using the present and future value formula. You might perceive one is more valuable than the other, but how confident are you in your answer? Are you as confident as the previous problems?

Using the present and future value formula, we find that the first payout of Project B is $476.19 and the second payout of Project B is $1,088.43, which means the net present value of the project is $476.19 + $1,088.43 – $1,000 = $564.62. Project B barely has a higher net present value. We doubt that your intuition alone—anyone's intuition—has enough precision to get the right answer. In any event, using the present and future value formula provides a relatively easy way to confidently answer questions like this. What would you do if you could finance both projects?

Comparing Multiple Contracts

Even your favorite NFL players—and any other athlete—can be entrepreneurial. Consider a star, rookie quarterback who is considering the three-year contracts with signing bonuses listed in Table 3.1. Assume an interest rate of 5 percent. Which team offers the best contract in terms of its net present value?

Once again, our intuitions are not helpful to compare these contracts. We might realize that the Jets and Colts offer very similar contracts, but without a clear winner. And we might realize that the Titans offer a higher signing bonus than the Jets and the Colts, but a smaller second year salary. It isn't clear how the magnitudes of those differences compare. Similarly, the Patriots offer the highest signing bonus, the lowest first year salary, and meager second and third year salaries.

Table 3.1 The present value of NFL contracts (in millions USD)

	Jets	Colts	Titans	Patriots
Signing bonus	$1	$1	$2	$3
First year salary	$.5	$.5	$.5	$.25
Second year salary	$1	$2	$.5	$1
Third year salary	$3	$ 2	$2	$2

Using the present and future value formula, you will find that the Jets, Colts, Titans, and Patriots offer your star quarterback contracts equal to $4.9 million, $5.0 million, $4.6 million, and $5.8 million, respectively. Now we can say—with much more confidence—that the Patriots are offering a better deal.

Indefinite and Definite Future Incomes

Alright, what about endowing a chaired professorship for your favorite professor? We need to consider how much money we need today to equal an indefinite stream of income that equals an annual payout, that is, the professor's annual salary. Assume that the chaired professorship entails an annual salary of $150,000, it includes benefits, and it is paid at the end of each year.

The problem becomes what is the present value of an indefinite number of yearly payments of $150,000? Assume the interest rate is 5 percent. Formally, we write this as $PV = \dfrac{\$150,000}{1.05} + \dfrac{\$150,000}{1.05^2} + \dfrac{\$150,000}{1.05^3} + \cdots + \dfrac{\$150,000}{1.05^n}$. While such a sum is technically solvable, it becomes very cumbersome, very quickly. There is a shortcut, but before we reveal it, note two things. First, the first term—which equals $142,857.14—is the largest as every subsequent term is divided by a larger number given the additional year. Second, and similarly, the very last term—where the time period is n—becomes a negligible amount. That is, we value the present value of that payout as close to nothing because it is so far away in time.

The shortcut requires a recognition of these factors and the following formula: $PV = \dfrac{FV}{i}$. Thus, if we want our dear professor to have $150,000 every year for the remainder of his or her life—and for the lives of the subsequent holders of that chair—divide $150,000 by the 5 percent interest rate. This equals $3,000,000. That's not too costly to honor the memory of your favorite professor!

Here is one final example for you budding entrepreneurs out there. Imagine you are considering the purchase of new machinery for your business or the expansion of your existing factories. Each of these projects is expensive, but you expect a yearly return for the foreseeable future, say the next 10 years. Are such projects worth the investment?

We can think about this question with the present and future value formula—our old friend. Let's say you are considering an expansion, and that it costs \$10,000,000 to expand, but you expect \$2,000,000 in revenue every year for the next 10 years. Is the machine worthwhile? To answer we equate the present cost with the future stream of expected income. Thus, $\$10,000,000 = \dfrac{\$2,000,000}{(1+i)} + \dfrac{\$2,000,000}{(1+i)^2} + \dfrac{\$2,000,000}{(1+i)^3} + \cdots + \dfrac{\$2,000,000}{(1+i)^{10}}$. Notice what our interest rate now tells us; it tells us the exact interest rate that equates the present cost of the machinery with the expected revenue. This rate is known as the *internal rate of return*, and it is the rate at which we would break even.

This equation is also quite cumbersome to solve; any internal rate of return calculator can help. We find that the internal rate of return is approximately 15 percent. While this might seem like a decent return, we also want to know the opportunity cost of that investment. For example, if you financed it with a loan at any interest rate above 15 percent, the project would cost more than its worth.

Inflation Hawks Needn't Worry

Yet another way to understand how interest rates work is to consider how inflation—the decline in the value of money that leads to a higher price level—influences the value of loans and debt. If Tony lends Larry money to start a bourbon business, and he expects \$5,000 in five years, Tony is perfectly willing and able to make the loan under these circumstances. Imagine, however, that right after Tony and Larry sign the contract, the United States goes to war. Wars are expensive, and analysts expect the rate of inflation to increase to 5 percent. Indeed, over the next five years, the inflation rate does increase to 5 percent! When Larry and Tony meet again to settle the contract, Larry gives Tony \$5,000. Does Tony value that \$5,000 the same way as what he initially expected?

A moment's reflection suggests the answer is no. To see why, note that what Tony (and Larry) is most concerned with as the lender (and as the borrower) is r, the *real* interest rate. This rate is a measure of a person's command over real goods. In all of the examples above, for example, we implicitly used real interest rates. That is, the interest rate showed how a person's real wealth changed over time. These rates were also *nominal* rates, or *i*, in that they described the real rate people were interested in. In those cases, $r = i$.

The situation changes as we consider a positive rate of inflation, π, like the situation with Tony and Larry. As the rate of inflation becomes positive, it wedges between the real and nominal rates and breaks the equality. Indeed, as we hold nominal rates constant—these are the rates used to establish contracts that are costly to change and slow to adjust— the real interest rate necessarily falls below the nominal rate: $r < i$ when $\pi > 0$. The Fisher equation—named after economist Irving Fisher— summarizes this logic: the real interest rate equals the nominal rate minus the rate of inflation: $r = i - \pi$.

The 5 percent Tony expected to receive erodes as the rate of inflation rises; he expected 5 percent but it fell to 0 percent. The 5 percent Larry expected to pay also changes; it falls to 0 percent. This example shows that when changes in the rate of inflation are unexpected, lenders are worse off and borrowers are better off. This is one of the economic problems that unexpected inflation poses.

To decrease the impact of inflation, lenders form expectations about the future rate of inflation. If both Tony and Larry expect an inflation rate of 5 percent, Tony—who wants a real return of 5 percent—would not lend his funds at any nominal interest rate below 10 percent. Similarly, if Larry really wants to buy bourbon barrels, he would be willing to offer a higher nominal interest rate.

Inflation-adjusted bonds provide another way to hedge against future changes in inflation. These are bonds where the principal and interest payments change as the inflation rate changes. So, even if changes in inflation are wholly unexpected, you can acquire these kinds of bonds to compensate for the losses due to inflation. In 2022, for example, many savers purchased I series savings bonds precisely because they promised high nominal rates of interest to cover the rapidly rising price of gasoline, food, electricity, and other goods.

Figure 3.2 shows the consumer price index for urban consumers— a standard measure of inflation—in terms of percent change from a year ago.

Figure 3.2 *Consumer price index for all urban consumers, 1948 to 2023*

Source: FRED database using fredr.

Throughout the first half of 2022, this price index consistently reported an inflation rate above 8 percent. Rates continued upward, much as they did during the 1970s, when high rates of inflation wreaked havoc on lenders.

CHAPTER 4

The Economics and Information of Interest

With a basic understanding of interest rates, we can tease out some important implications and glean additional information about the general state of economic activity. Despite the simple examples of Chapter 3, interest rates are rarely constant for long periods of time; they can change daily, by the hour, and by the nanosecond. We now focus on why such changes occur and what they mean.

Interest Rates Are More Than Indicators of Time Preference

Interest rates are important sources of information not just about the value of financial assets, but about the state of economic activity. That is, by looking at changes in interest rates, you should be able to explain why those changes occurred and better understand how those changes influence economic activity.

Consider, for example, changes in the 10-year treasury rate—the yield on 10-year treasury bills from the U.S. government. Figure 4.1 shows this series. You might think the risk of default is a relevant factor, especially for bonds. Of course, no financial asset is completely free of risk, but a U.S. Treasury obligation (note, bill, or bond) is one of the least risky assets you might acquire; this is particularly because the U.S. government can use tax revenue to pay off debt or, if need be, it can create new money to pay bondholders. The point is that change in the riskiness of these bonds cannot explain yield changes.

Whereas the riskiness of U.S. treasuries is not that relevant, what caused the 10-year yield to rise, for example, during the 1970s? Recall Figure 3.2 on the consumer price index and our discussion of the Fisher

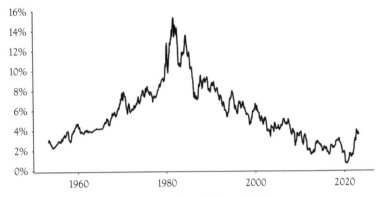

Figure 4.1 10-year treasury yields, 1953 to 2023

Source: FRED database using fredr.

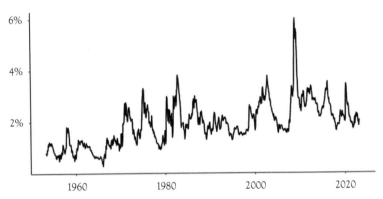

Figure 4.2 Spread on 10-year Baa and U.S. treasury bond yields, 1953 to 2023

Source: FRED database using fredr.

equation in Chapter 3. We realized that nominal interest rates follow changes in the rate of inflation. And if you search through the history of the 1970s in the United States, you will quickly discover inflation rates were particularly high. To maintain an expected real return in the face of inflation, lenders and bondholders required higher interest rates or yields.

Speaking of risk, consider Figure 4.2, which shows the spread—the *difference* between yields—on 10-year Baa corporate bonds and 10-year treasury bonds. When this series rises, it suggests the Baa bonds are riskier relative to treasury bonds. In this way, it becomes a better measure of risk than each of the individual series. The spread shows how risk influences interest rates. For example, when firms are less likely to pay their debts, people might require additional compensation, which leads to higher interest rates.

The growth of this series in 2008—and its peak—indicates the extent of risk and uncertainty during the global financial crisis between 2007 and 2009—a topic we will return to throughout the text. Also, note the relative decline in risk during the COVID-19 crisis; this series suggests that crisis was unrelated to financial markets.

These Rates Might Mean Something, but They Fluctuate

We can make inferences from how we view interest rates and as we compare rates from different issuers. Before we noted that the spread between 10-year Baa and U.S. Treasury bonds suggests the riskiness associated with default. Similarly, we can view multiple series to get a better idea of how risk changes over different categories of bonds, like bonds issued by municipalities and different types of corporations. Figure 4.3 shows the comparison in yields between 20-year treasury bonds, Moody's Aaa and Baa bonds (with an average maturity of 20 years), and the average rate for 30-year fixed rate mortgages.

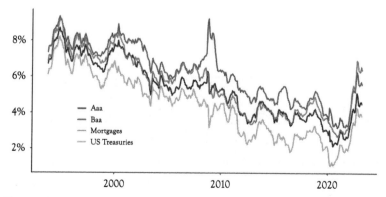

Figure 4.3 The risk structure of interest rates, 1993 to 2023: yields on bonds from different issuers

Source: FRED database using fredr.

One of the most important stylized facts or general features of these yields is what economists refer to as the risk structure of interest rates. This structure refers to the way in which bonds from relatively low-risk sources have consistently low yields relative to bonds from relatively high-risk sources. Thus, treasury bonds—some of the most risk-free and highly liquid assets available—consistently have lower yields relative to Aaa corporate bonds, which are lower than Baa bonds and mortgage rates. Junk bonds and municipal bonds are often much more risky and less liquid, so they have some of the highest yields. Municipal governments want to spend—and they can only tax so much and have no ability to print money like the federal government can. But they long enjoyed tax exemptions that decreased their yields holding risk and liquidity constant. Moreover, some muni bonds come from dedicated revenue streams, so they are less subject to capricious local politics. Unlike firms that issue Aaa bonds, firms that issue junk bonds have poor or unknown reputations. They sell debt into the market when they cannot acquire sufficient external finance from commercial banks, an example of the lemons problem discussed in more detail later.

We can summarize this cacophony of outcomes by considering the *risk premium* it would take to acquire additional risk, be it risk of default, illiquidity, or taxation.

During periods of crisis—financial or otherwise—people often value the relative safety of treasury bonds over corporate and municipal bonds. For instance, Figure 4.4 shows the spread on Aaa and Baa

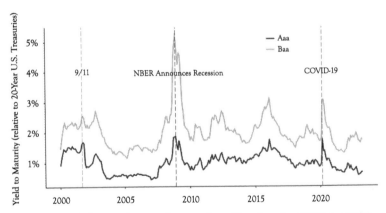

Figure 4.4 Flights to Aaa and away from Baa bonds, 2000 to 2023

Source: FRED database using fredr.

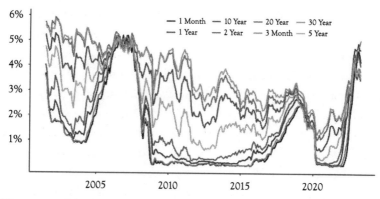

Figure 4.5 The term structure of interest rates, 2001 to 2023: yields on treasuries of different maturities

Source: FRED database using fredr.

corporate bonds (relative to 20-year treasury bonds). Note the spikes after September 11, 2001, the Great Recession of 2007 to 2009, and the onset of COVID-19 in March and April 2020. During the first two crises, a so-called *flight to quality* occurred as investors sold riskier forms of debt to buy treasuries. During the COVID-19 crisis, in contrast, yields on all types of bonds increased temporarily due to the uncertain economic effects of the virus, which was inaccurately portrayed as *novel* during the initial phase of the pandemic.

Furthermore, note that if we examine the yields on different bonds from the same borrower, we expect the risk of default to remain similar. In this way, we can derive the term structure of interest rates, or how interest rates vary over bond maturity. Figure 4.5 shows this structure with U.S. treasuries. Notice how yields are consistently higher as bond maturity lengthens.

The term structure of interest rates shows that investors are willing to acquire longer-term bonds but generally only when they are compensated by higher yields. These yields also contain important information about what might happen to economic activity in the short term, a topic we will return to later in this chapter.

The Market Process and Market Clearing Prices Clarify

So, what is it that might explain *changes* in these rates? Generally, any condition that changes when people want to acquire funds and when people want to lend funds constitutes a relevant factor. This applies to your grandmother and to Elon Musk alike. Surely many factors explain these changes, but supply and demand are most consistently relevant.

Recall that prices emerge from the coordinating process of market participants, that is, buyers and sellers. Whenever those groups meet and are willing to exchange, the myriad bids and offers coalesce to form prices. Furthermore, prices change as the conditions of supply and demand change. This insight provides the basic method to think about how interest rates change.

To start, we can examine the market for loanable funds, which is comprised of separate but related markets for credit, loans, and bonds. We define the demand for loanable funds as the relationship between the amount of funds borrowers want to obtain and the sacrifice they are willing to make to obtain those funds. Like the demand for every other good, this logic suggests there is a negative relationship between the amount of funds and the sacrifice made, that is, *interest* paid or the opportunity cost of a loan. Figure 4.6 shows the demand for loanable funds. Notice that the curve is downward sloping.

Obviously, when interest rates are high, fewer consumers and businesses will want to borrow. Vacations, automobiles, and new factories become more costly the higher rates are. As rates decrease, consumers and businesses want to borrow more because the overall cost (purchase prices plus financing costs) of the goods they want goes down. So, the quantity of loans demanded at 1 percent is higher than at 5 or 10 percent.

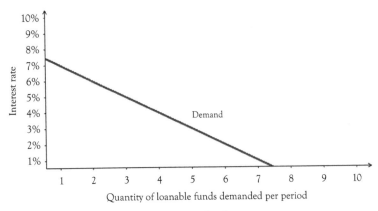

Figure 4.6 *The demand for loanable funds*

The supply of loanable funds constitutes the other major portion of the credit market. The more reward lenders receive, all else constant, the more they are willing to lend, suggesting the supply of credit, like the supply of other goods, has an upward sloping curve like in Figure 4.7.

For example, if borrowers are willing to pay an interest of 3 percent at the most, lenders will lend three units (millions of dollars, billions of yen, etc.) of loanable funds.

With that logic in mind, note that borrowers (consumers) want lower interest rates (prices) and lenders (sellers) want higher interest rates (prices). Through the myriad negotiations of many borrowers and lenders, the market for loans clears just as the market for other goods does. To visualize this, consider the supply and demand conditions together as they *both* are needed to explain the interest rates we might observe. Figure 4.8 shows these curves together, which is a graphical depiction of the market for loanable funds.

Plan coordination happens at the prevailing rate of interest or, generally, where supply and demand intersect, approximately 4 percent in Figure 4.8. This is the interest rate where the market *clears*. If a lender were to ask for a rate higher than 4 percent in Figure 4.8, the amount of funds supplied would be larger than the amount of funds requested. Lenders are willing to offer a higher amount of funds as it comes with a higher reward; however, borrowers are less willing to take the loan as it comes with a higher cost. If that situation were to persist, it would put downward pressure on interest rates; lenders would begin to scale back

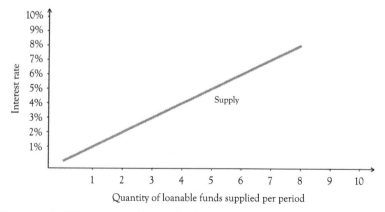

Figure 4.7 *The supply of loanable funds*

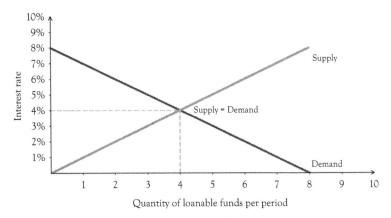

Figure 4.8 The market for loanable funds

their offer and lower rates. As that happens, more borrowers acquire funds as they are willing to take the loan at lower rates. This process continues until the market clearing rate is achieved.

Similarly, if a lender offered a rate that was lower than 4 percent in Figure 4.8, the amount of loans requested would be larger than the amount of funds available. Borrowers would expect low rates, which encourages additional borrowings; lenders would cut back as they expect a smaller reward. This situation pushes interest rates back up to the market clearing rate.

At this point, you might be wondering how it is that interest rates change frequently, as shown earlier, and how it is that rates tend to clear the market. These are not mutually exclusive categories as the following sections clarify. They deal with changes in the underlying supply and demand conditions: when those conditions change, the market clearing rate changes too.

Rates Move in the Bond Market and in All Loanable Funds Markets

The supply and demand for bonds provide a relatively easy way to better understand the market for loanable funds. Recall that a bond—in addition to the fancy paper that specifies a face value—is a promise borrowers make to pay lenders in some future period. And that the present discounted value of a bond today is equal to its face value divided by interest, which also equals the prevailing market price: $PV_{bond} = \dfrac{Face\ Value}{(1+i)^t} = P_B.$ Following this formula, we see that the price of a bond—its present value—is inversely related to the interest on the bond and *vice versa*.

Once we recognize the demand for bonds is the relationship between how many bonds we want to obtain and how much we are willing to pay for them, and the supply of bonds is the relationship between how many bonds we are willing to sell and what we are willing to sell them for, we can discuss some of the factors that influence supply and demand, respectively.

Each of the following conditions increases the demand for bonds:

- An increase in income
- A decrease in expected inflation
- A decrease in expected interest rates
- An increase in the expected return due to either of the following:
  ○ An increase in liquidity
  ○ A decrease in relative risk

Each of the following conditions increases the supply of bonds:

- An improvement in business conditions
- An increase in expected inflation
- An increase in government deficits

Each follows economic principles, but it won't hurt to review.

The Demand for Bonds

Income and Bond Yields

As income rises, people have more money to spend on goods they expect will improve their well-being. Bonds fall into that category of goods.

When large portions of a population experience rising incomes— during periods of economic growth, for example—we should expect to see an increase in the demand for bonds. This increase in demand, say for five-year bonds with a face value of $1,000, raises the price of bonds and

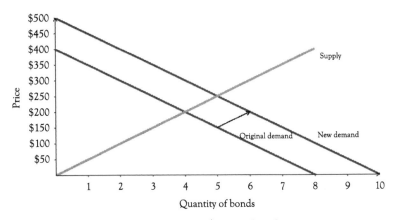

Figure 4.9 The market for five-year $1,000 bonds

the quantity of bonds purchased and sold, all else equal, as indicated in
Figure 4.9.

Expected Return and Bond Yields

Another relevant factor that influences bond prices and yields is the
expected return on bonds. This return indicates how inflation-adjusted
wealth changes. Any factor that raises the expected return on a bond suggests more people would want to purchase a bond, all else equal.

The expected return of a bond—like the expected return of anything
else—is *relative*. That is, the return you expect to receive from a bond
depends on the return you might expect to receive from owning a stock,
another bond, or lending the same amount of funds to your sister. If the
expected return in the stock market rises, for example, the expected *relative* return on bonds falls.

Liquidity is also important. As you develop expectations that an asset
is easily and cheaply saleable, it is said to be liquid. As liquidity rises, all
else equal, the demand for a bond rises because the bond is more like
money and less like land or art or other assets that can be costly and time
consuming to sell.

Expected Inflation and Bond Yields

Another factor that influences the expected return on a bond is the
expected inflation rate. The logic here follows from the Fisher equation.
Just as people adjust their borrowing and lending behaviors as they expect

higher rates of inflation, they can also adjust their purchases of bonds. As the expected rate of inflation rises—and the value of future dollars falls— the real value of bonds falls too. The idea is that a potential bondholder faces the following question, "Why would I buy a bond with a face value that I expect will decline due to inflation?" Rising expected inflation lowers the present value of bonds. Thus, the demand for bonds fall, as does its price and quantity purchased and sold. Of course, yields rise.

Expected Interest Rates and Bond Yields

Now imagine that interest rates change after you've purchased a bond. For example, imagine you purchased a 10-year bond with a $1,000 face value at a 5 percent interest rate. If the interest rate doubles in the fifth year, consider how the opportunity cost of lending has changed. That is, it has increased. But as your funds are tied up—they are in the hands of the bond issuer—you cannot make any adjustments. If you were to purchase additional bonds, however, you would realize the present value of a bond is lower; thus, demand and bond prices will fall.

The Supply of Bonds

Business Conditions and Bond Yields

Say you were living through a period of economic growth like the 1990s. You might surmise that if such trends continued, you could do something to take advantage of it. That is, you could start a new business, you could expand your existing workforce, or build new factories. These options, however, are costly, and you might not have the funds to pay for them. As we already know, bonds help coordinate borrowers and lenders, so we expect to see the supply of bonds rising during periods of economic growth, which leads to falling prices and rising yields, all else equal. Figure 4.10 shows this relationship in the market for bonds, for example, a five-year bond with a face value of $1,000.

Expected Inflation and Bond Yields

As the expected inflation rate rises, lenders realize they might receive less than what they wanted and start to cut back on lending; however,

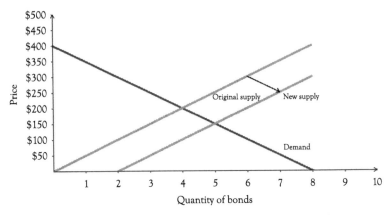

Figure 4.10 The bond market and improving business conditions

borrowers rejoice. That is, they realize the real cost of paying what they promised will be less than what they anticipated. All else equal, this means that individuals, firms, and governments who are interested in issuing bonds, that is, borrowing to fund current projects, will issue additional bonds. The supply of bonds rises, the price of bonds falls, the quantity of bonds rises, and bond yields rise.

Government Budgets and Bond Yields

Municipal, state, and federal governments issue bonds to finance various projects. If a city government wants to improve its road network, it might sell new bonds to finance that construction; if a federal government wants to go to war, it can issue bonds to fight that war. As such, these operations—and its effects on the government budget—influences the market for bonds. Thus, the supply of bonds increases when governments tend to run deficits, and, as a result, prices fall and yields rise.

Applying Supply and Demand

The two following scenarios help to better explain the sophisticated tool kit of supply and demand, and they give us additional insight into how bond markets work. Each scenario follows from the supply and demand conditions we discussed earlier, and they analyze changing business conditions and a change in expected inflation.

Do Bond Yields Rise or Fall During Periods of Economic Growth?

To answer this question, recognize that bond yields respond in different ways to business cycles. As people experience higher incomes during periods of economic growth, the supply and demand for bonds rises. The ultimate effect on bond yields is therefore theoretically unclear because additional demand tends to lower yields, whereas additional supply tends to raise yields. Thus, whether bond yields rise or fall during periods of growth depends on which factor is larger. If bond yields tend to rise (fall) during periods of economic growth, the change in supply (demand) dominates. Figure 4.11 shows the real GDP growth rate (measured on the right axis) and the 10-year treasury yield (measured on the left-hand-side axis). These series show that bond yields tend to rise during periods of growth and fall during recessions, which suggests the change in supply is larger than the change in demand.

Do Bond Yields Rise or Fall as Expected Inflation Rises?

Changes in expected inflation influence the supply and demand of bonds; that is, there are two effects that develop simultaneously. Whereas the demand for bonds decreases as inflation expectations rise, the supply of bonds rises. Review the logic earlier that follows the Fisher equation for clarification. These two effects reinforce one

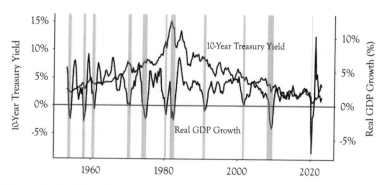

Figure 4.11 The relationship between business cycles and bond yields

Source: FRED database using fredr.

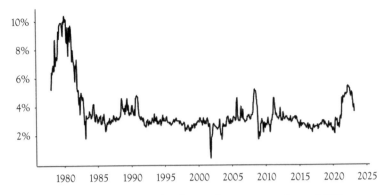

Figure 4.12 Expected rate of inflation from survey data, 1978 to 2023

Source: FRED database using fredr.

another. That is, bond yields tend to rise (fall) when inflation expectations rise (fall) because the demand for bonds decreases and the supply of bonds increases. Comparing Figure 4.12, which shows the University of Michigan's survey of inflation expectations, with the yields in Figure 4.11, we should recognize this theoretical relationship is borne out in available data.

Consider the early 1980s—where inflation expectations fell after the relatively tumultuous 1970s. The logic of supply and demand suggests (1) the demand for bonds rises (which lowers yields) and (2) the supply of bonds will fall (which lowers yields).

There Is Information About Current Risk

Recall our previous notes about the term structure of interest rates and Figure 4.5. This structure holds that the risks associated with default and liquidity are constant, and it explicitly examines the influence the length of maturation has on bond yields. In the case of Figure 4.5—where all of the bonds are treasury bonds—there is not a significant difference in the risks associated with U.S. governments over the next 30 years. Yet, yields still change: some yields tend to be lower than others, and some yields tend to closely resemble other yields. Discerning what this structure means is what we want to figure out.

Consider the yields on one- and five-year bonds—in Figure 4.13—and notice the following:

- Yields move together.
- Short-term yields are more volatile than long-term yields.
- Long-term yields tend to be higher than short-term yields.

Why do these three regularities generally hold? Note first the similarity between purchasing multiple short-term bonds and purchasing a single long-term bond from the same issuer. With U.S. Treasury bonds, for example, the difference between five one-year bonds and one five-year bond is negligible. That is, if you wanted to buy five one-year bonds—one after the other over the next five years—you wouldn't be better or worse than if you were to buy a single five-year bond. These similarities suggest an *expectations* hypothesis; that is, investors develop similar expectations about the yields on short- and long-term bonds. With such expectations, the yields on short- and long-term bonds will tend to equalize.

Using one- and five-year treasuries to clarify, the expectations hypothesis suggests that the current five-year yield equals the average of the one-year yields over the next five years: $i_{51} = \dfrac{i_{11} + i_{12} + \cdots + i_{15}}{5}$, where the first number in the subscript refers to the length of maturity and the second refers to the current year. For example, imagine if you knew the one-year treasury yields over the next five years: they are 4.5, 4.2, 4.0,

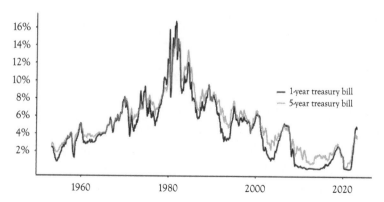

Figure 4.13 *The term structure with one- and five-year treasuries*

Source: FRED database using fredr.

3.5, and 4.6 percent. The average of these yields is 4.16 percent, which suggests the current yield on a five-year treasury equals 4.16 percent.

For another example, and to see whether this theory provides a relevant description of bond yields, let's look at one- and five-year yields over the last five years. The five-year yield in August 2016 was 1.13, which suggests it equals the average of the one-year yields (for August) in 2016, 2017, 2018, 2019, and 2020. These rates were 0.57, 1.23, 2.43, 1.77, and 0.13; thus, the average of these numbers equals 1.22. Not bad. We are looking backward in time rather than using expectations, which is partly why there is a difference; also, investors might not always consider these bonds to be perfect substitutes.

In any event, this aspect of the term structure leads to an important tool in the economic analysis of money and banking—*the yield curve*. This curve is a way to gather information about current—and potentially future—economic activity as it shows the relationship between current yields (on a vertical axis) and the time to maturity (on a horizontal axis). Figure 4.14 shows three yield curves for U.S. Treasury bonds on three Mondays in September 2021 (September 6, 13, and 20).

The general implication of Figure 4.14 is that we expect interest rates to rise, given the upward sloping nature of current yield curves. Not only should we expect rates to rise over the next couple years, they might level off at a consistently higher rate over the next couple decades.

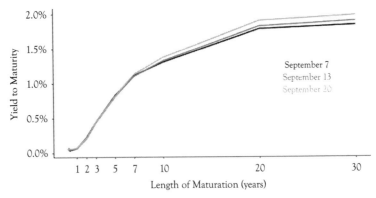

Figure 4.14 Changes in the U.S. yield curve in September 2021

Source: FRED database using fredr.

This construction of the expectations hypothesis allows us to explain the first and second stylized facts of the term structure. That is, short- and long-term interest rates travel together; if the short-term yields rise or fall, so will the long-term yields. Similarly, short-term yields are more volatile than long-term yields. The expectations hypothesis suggests that the average of the short-term rates smooths out such fluctuations and moves those yields closer to the long-term yield.

The expectations hypothesis, however, cannot explain the third stylized fact, but the liquidity premium hypothesis can help. This hypothesis extends the expectations hypothesis, but it accounts for differences in risk between these bonds—especially because of the risks that change over longer periods of time, namely inflation and interest rate risk. That is, the longer you hold a bond, the more likely the initial rate of inflation and/or the interest rate will increase, decreasing its market price. Thus, the longer a bond takes to mature, the more uncertain you will be about its present discounted value. This uncertainty suggests that to consider these short and long bonds substitutes, investors will need some compensation. That compensation is the *liquidity premium*.

To account for this premium and extend the expectations hypothesis from above, we should recognize that the current long-term yield equals the sum of (1) the average of the short-term yields over n years and (2) the risk premium, rp_n. If rp_n rises with n, then it offers a neat explanation for stylized Fact 3 and why long-term yields tend to be higher than otherwise equal short-term bonds.

And, Perhaps, a Crystal Ball

A final note on yield curves and the term structure is now in order. We can use the information from these curves to predict when an economy is at higher risk of entering a recession. That is really important information to know—or at the very least be able to contemplate. If you are about to expand your business, you might want to have some information about whether customers might want to buy your goods. If you expect the economy is going to go through a recession—a reduction in per capita real output—over the next year, you might decide to wait on that new project.

Recall that when yield curves are upward sloping—which they usually are—we expect interest rates to rise, as they do during expansions as explained above. Similarly, when they are downward sloping, or *inverted* as is sometimes said, we expect interest rates to fall, as they do during recessions. So, by analyzing yield curves—and how they change over time—we can develop predictions about how interest rates might change. In particular, when long-term yields fall below short-term yields, something important is happening. When this inversion happens, markets predict an oncoming recession. The intuition is that when short-term rates are high relative to long-term rates, people expect long-term bonds will appreciate in price as interest rates decline in the near future. Figure 4.15 shows a one-year lagged term spread—the difference between 10- and three-year treasury yields—with recession shading to demonstrate the predictive power of *inverted* yield curves.

Figure 4.15 shows that as the yield curve became inverted—when the term spread becomes negative—there tends to be a fall in the real growth rate a year later. This isn't a perfect predictor of future economic downturns—could anyone have predicted COVID-19, or that it would lead to economically disastrous lockdowns?—but it is a good leading indicator of regular business cycle recessions. That is, the use of yield curves—and knowing when they become inverted—can predict relatively poor future economic activity.

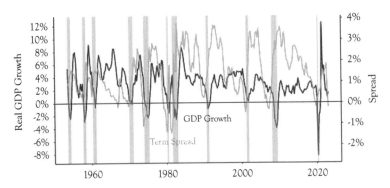

Figure 4.15 One-year lagged term spread and real GDP growth

Source: FRED database using fredr.

CHAPTER 5

Risk

Risk encompasses the good, the bad, and everything in between. Everyone must accept some risk, but financial markets can help you to manage it. Nobody wants to wreck a car or lose savings during a stock market crash. Yet, people rejoice when they hit all the green lights or ride a rally. Rationally assessing, pricing, and trading risk are key functions of financial markets and institutions.

Speaking of Risk, It's Everywhere

Risk, which includes positive gains and negative losses, pervades all. Investors want the rewards but not the losses, but the two cannot be separated. Investors assume risk in exchange for commensurate reward. If you've ever purchased insurance; if you ever worked for a brothel or became an economics and business major; and if you ever wondered why a coffee shop sells multiple products, you are familiar with risk. People buy insurance to cover the costs associated with possible future events; sex workers find that working for a brothel eliminates some of the risks they face regarding violence, payment, and sexually transmitted diseases; students hedge future employment risk by majoring in economics and business, especially when they don't know what they want to do after graduation; coffee shops and cafes sell multiple products to spread the risk of particular items not selling well.

Merchants, Brothel Madams, and Wall Street Bros All Bear Risk

Risk is not a new problem and neither is its mitigation. Centuries ago, for example, Maghribi merchants in the Mediterranean faced risk when shipping goods. Prices might change, goods might be stolen—by the crew or by pirates—or bad weather could temporarily delay a voyage or end in the total loss of ship and goods. Cargoes could spoil, and supercargoes, the merchants' agents, might commit fraud. Merchants could have earned more than what they expected, lost everything, or anything in between.

Sex workers and their clients face risk too. People want to buy or sell sexual goods, but the quality of those goods varies. Any given exchange could result in successful interactions—payment received and adequate goods rendered—or it could result in disappointment, theft, abuse, death, or, in many countries, fines or imprisonment.

Wall Street veterans also face risk, or variability of return. They might channel funds into projects that make themselves or their clients wealthy, or they could lose it all.

Risk Is in Our Investments and Prices

Risk pervades financial markets. As Figure 5.1 shows, the price of Bitcoin—a type of cryptocurrency—fluctuates wildly. Once you purchase Bitcoin, you expose yourself to the risk that Bitcoin could rise or fall in value. Buying Bitcoin in late 2016 or early 2017—in hindsight—was a good bet if you sold before mid-2018. Its price increased by over 1,500 percent.

Compare the changes in the price of Bitcoin to home prices—measured by the S&P/Case-Schiller U.S. national home price index in Figure 5.2.

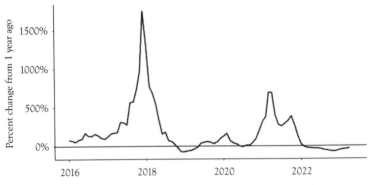

Figure 5.1 Changes in the price of Bitcoin, 2016 to 2023

Source: Coinbase Bitcoin [CBBTCUSD]. FRED database using fredr.

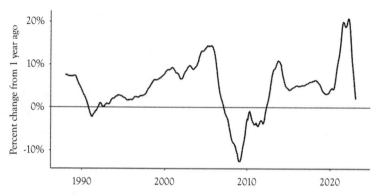

Figure 5.2 Changes in the S&P/Case-Shiller U.S. national home price index, 1988 to 2023

Source: FRED database using fredr.

To make the comparison more intelligible, note the range in values. Whereas Bitcoin ranged from $120 (in January 2015) to $67,510 (in November 2021), the home price index ranged from 63.9 (in January 1987) to 279.8 (in December 2021). Thus, the larger percent changes for Bitcoin prices means it is risky because of much higher variations in returns. In addition to the opportunities a house provides to build a family, to entertain, and to expand wealth, houses are relatively stable investments because the price tomorrow is likely to be similar to the price today. Bitcoin provides a larger return but only at the expense of more risk of large losses.

Risk Is Idiosyncratic and Systematic

Bitcoin and houses—and their respective price changes—suggest we should know more about different kinds of risks. Bitcoin aficionados and home buyers face sectoral risks, or risks that influence the value of all goods in a particular market. The potential for China—or any other country—to ban Bitcoin influences the value of all Bitcoin as it influences its demand. Moreover, that change might not have any noticeable influence on home prices. Similarly, a housing bubble—whether it is forming or bursting—primarily affects home prices, but not Bitcoin prices. To the extent these goods are substitutes, however, changing market conditions for one will influence market conditions in the other. If China

were to ban Bitcoin, holders of Bitcoin might use their Bitcoin to purchase houses, which would greatly increase the demand—and prices—of
homes. More likely, though, they will convert their Bitcoin into a wide
variety of assets, thus influencing their respective prices.

Investment opportunities also face idiosyncratic risks, whereby the
value of a specific asset rises or falls despite the general market trend. For
example, home prices across some region might be on the rise, but particular homes might rise even further, or fall, depending on local conditions,
like if a new school or a brothel opened next door. Risk might also be
systematic, where many individuals and firms fare well or poorly together.
If the price of gasoline rises, for example, all firms will face higher costs.
Whether systematic or idiosyncratic, risk is problematic, but its bite can
be managed!

Thank Goodness, Risk Is Manageable

Venetian merchants and shipowners were keenly aware of the risks
they faced. They couldn't do much about the weather—or the dragons
thought to inhabit the ends of the world—but they could write contracts, form coalitions to share risk, and develop reputations for fair deal-
ing (Greif 1989).

One of the ways sex workers—men and women—avoid risk is to
gather information about prospective clients and/or by contracting with
brothels to enforce appropriate behavior (Logan 2017; Schrager 2019).
Sex workers might share some of their earnings with the madame (or
pimp), but they do so to reduce the probability of being beaten up, stiffed
by a client, or contracting a sexually transmitted disease. They face less
risk but also less return.

Many financial instruments reduce risk too. Insurance lowers the cost
of unexpected, harmful events in exchange for periodic premium payments. Forward and futures contracts allow people to lock in future prices
today. Mortgage-backed securities—some of the most maligned instruments after the 2007–2009 Great Recession—pool risks by combining
multiple mortgages into one instrument.

We Can Measure Risk

Investors evaluate projects by considering likely outcomes and associated risks. Projects entail considerations of a net payout (benefits and costs) and a probability of success (risk). Imagine that Project A earns a net reward of $1,000, with a 50 percent chance of success, and $0 otherwise; Project B earns a net reward of $1,000, with a 45 percent chance of success, and $0 otherwise. Intuitively, the choice is a no-brainer in favor of Project A. Often, though, the decision is not obvious, so it is useful to think through why Project A might be superior. Project A might be preferred because it has an expected value of $500 ($1,000 * 0.5), while Project B has an expected value of only $450 ($1,000 * 0.45). The expected value of any opportunity, investment, or project is the sum of each possible reward multiplied by its probability of success. While Project A has a higher expected value, it is not necessarily the better option. Investors might also evaluate projects based on the dispersion of risk or its variance. If an investor cares more about the dispersion of risk—not just the likely outcome—B is the better option. Any project's variance—measured in dollars squared—measures the dispersion of risk, which we calculate by: (1) finding the expected value, (2) taking the difference between each of the possible payouts and the expected value, (3) squaring those differences, (4) multiplying each result by its respective probability, and (5) summing each product. Any project's standard deviation—measured in dollars—is easier to interpret and is found by taking the square root of the variance.

For example, the standard deviation of Project A—which has equally likely payouts of $1,000 and $0 and an expected value of $500—equals: $\sqrt{.5*(\$1,000-\$500)^2+.5*(\$0-\$500)^2} = \sqrt{125,000+125,000} = \$500$. The standard deviation of Project B—which has a 45 percent chance of earning $1,000, a 55 percent chance of earning $0, and an expected value of $450—equals: $\sqrt{.45*(\$1,000-\$450)^2+.55*(\$0-\$450)^2} = \sqrt{136,125+111,375} = \$497.49$. Project B is less risky as it has a smaller variance and standard deviation.

The choice between A and B, therefore, is not as clear as you might have thought at first. If you value the project that typically has a higher reward, Project A is the winner. However, if you value the project that is less risky, Project B is the winner. For some investors, Project A might have a high enough reward to compensate the additional risk. Other investors might eschew Project A because they do not think the reward is enough to bear the risk.

These factors indicate there are likely to be cases where people choose projects not solely based on their relative expected values but also on their riskiness. Ultimately, these kinds of decisions are up to individual decision makers; they are subjective and depend on one's tolerance for risk relative to the reward.

Economic Calculation and Profits Follow Measurement

This way of assessing risk allows people to quantify the risks they face; it leads to a greater ability to evaluate and consider the kinds of projects people should pursue or accept. Quantifying these risks, aided by money prices, facilitates economic calculation. Should you go to college, and how much should you pay for it? Should you invest in Bitcoin, and when should you sell or buy more? Should you become a sex worker? These are all difficult questions people face, but they can use the logic of risk—and how to embrace it and minimize its costs—to improve their lives.

PART III

The Economics of Financial Markets

Given ever-present problems related to risk, uncertainty, and information, people strive for solutions. They write contracts and form intermediaries to pursue their goals. Unbeknownst to individuals minding their own business, the market process is at work, whereby competition rewards innovation and punishes waste. This selection process also works in financial transactions and makes our lives easier. For example, people can lend their funds and buy stocks with securities markets; people can mitigate wildly fluctuating commodity prices with a simple contract; people can buy goods abroad with foreign exchange markets; people can limit information asymmetry with insurance policies; people can save money for decades with banks.

CHAPTER 6

Securities Markets and Market Efficiency

Markets for financial securities—from long-term bonds to short-term commercial paper and from equities (common stocks) to hybrids (part bond, part stock)—make it easier to finance a firm's day-to-day operations or expand a *small cap* corporation into a Fortune 500 powerhouse. Securities markets match economic entities (corporations, governments, and, occasionally, individuals) that are looking for financing with people who have cash they wish to invest.

Common stocks offer promises to a future stream of income—like the bonds we discussed earlier—and some right to influence how the corporation is managed, and by whom. Stocks are salable, fungible, and they offer limited liability. That is, people can buy or sell as many or as few shares of stock as they want without being financially liable if the company goes bankrupt.

Roman Centurions and Dutch Merchants Faced the Same Problem

One of the earliest securities markets emerged in Rome to facilitate a bidding process initiated by the Roman government (Goetzmann 2017). Roman leaders realized their empire was becoming large and unwieldy, and that they could not collect enough tax revenue. So, they auctioned off the right to collect tax revenue to investors. The resulting contract was much like a government bond, except the investors who bought the collection rights, called tax *farmers*, did not have to worry about the government not servicing its bonds. Taxpayers paid their taxes to the tax farmers instead of to government tax collectors.

Securities markets emerged in Rome to help investors finance tax farming operations, which often entailed long expeditions and big upfront expenditures for food, clothes, weapons, horses, and so forth. Importantly, the shares people purchased for a particular expedition were salable, allowing investors to increase or decrease their risk exposure as their personal circumstances changed.

A thousand years after the fall of the Roman Empire, Dutch merchants faced a similar set of problems and developed similar solutions. In the early 1600s, they sought to profit from expanding trade but didn't have the requisite funds to launch endeavors that spanned the globe. They therefore formed joint stock companies like the Dutch East India Company that issued shares of stock to those who contributed upfront cash. The transferable shares of those companies traded in stock markets in cities like Amsterdam. An account of those markets penned in 1688 by Joseph de la Vega called *Confusion de Confusiones* reveals just how modern stock trading had already become.

We Face the Same Problems Today and Have the Same Solution

People today confront the same problems the Romans, the Dutch, and all other enterprising peoples have faced. Businesses do not always have sufficient funds to bring goods to market. Investors have cash to lend, but they are wary of borrowers or securities issuers who might take the money and run. Moreover, the two sides might not know who has money to invest or who stands in need of financing. Securities, and markets for them, reduce such problems by facilitating exchange.

Alphabet, Amazon, and all other large firms also need external financing help. Generally, they want to expand their businesses quickly, before competitors can take market share from them, but their free cash flow (revenues minus expenditures) is too small to do so. So they borrow from banks or issue securities—from short-term commercial paper to long term bonds to permanent common stocks. Investors are willing to pay the present value of the expected future stream of cash from the instrument. Figure 6.1 shows how the value of GameStop, a computer gaming retailer, has changed over time, as indicated by its daily closing stock price and volume of trades.

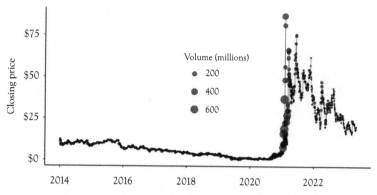

Figure 6.1 GameStop (GME), 2014 to 2023

Source: Yahoo Finance using quantmod R package.

Just as the market price for other goods changes based on changes in supply and demand, the market price for GME changes. If GameStop issued more stock, there would be more available, and its price would fall, *ceteris paribus* (all else equal). If GameStop were to become a less valuable company——as many investors over the last decade have believed——fewer people would want to purchase its stock, and its price would fall. Something clearly happened to increase the price of GME in early 2021; we will speak more about GameStop and why its stock price increased in 2020 and 2021 in Chapter 7.

A Problem Where Stocks Save the Day

Investors want to know if and when they should buy and sell specific stocks. Generally, investors should buy stock when they believe that its present value (PV) rises above the market price (P) and sell when they believe its PV falls below the prevailing price. Investors have different views of the *fair* value of stocks because they form different expectations about future earnings (profits) and because they form different expectations about risk, or in other words, because they use different discount factors.

A Familiar Logic

The present value formula is one heuristic to better understand this logic. Let the present value equal the prevailing price, P_o, the future value equal the prevailing price in the future, P_t, the interest rate equal i, and the period of time equal t. If, for example, an investor expects the price of GameStop stock (GME) to be \$300 in five years, $P_5 = \$300$, its P_o (when $i = 0.05$) is \$235.05. That is, if the price of GME today is greater than \$235.05, the investor should not buy because GME is more expensive than its present discounted value. The investor should buy, however, at any price below \$235.05.

Don't Forget Dividends

Many stocks pay dividends, D_t, or periodic (typically quarterly, but here annually) cash payments on each share of common stock. The present value formula still applies for these stocks but with a slight modification. Imagine GameStop, for example, issued a yearly \$50 dividend. The present discounted value of GME becomes a function of its future sales price—say \$300 like before—and the five \$50 dividend payments over the next five years: $P_0 = \dfrac{\$300}{(1+i)^t} + \dfrac{D_t}{(1+i)^t}$. Expanding the time periods, the present discounted value of GME with dividends is approximately

$$\frac{\$300}{(1+.05)^5} + \frac{\$50}{(1+.05)^1} + \frac{\$50}{(1+.05)^2} + \cdots + \frac{\$50}{(1+.05)^5} =$$

$$\$235.05 + \$47.61 + \$45.35 + \$43.19 + \$41.13 + \$39.17 = \$451.52$$

Note that the present discounted value of GME is substantially higher because not only has its share price increased, it has also paid \$250 per share to stockholders.

A More General Logic

A more general way to evaluate whether people should purchase stocks accounts for the *growth* of earnings over time, whether those earnings are retained by the corporation or paid out as dividends. Estimating an annual earnings growth rate, g, approximates this situation. The value of a stream of earnings, D_t, equals the expected earnings, D, multiplied by $(1 + g)^t$: $D_t = D * (1 + g)^t$. For example, if $g = 0.01$ and $D = \$50.00$, the present value of earnings (say, a dividend payment) in one year, D_1, equals

$$\$50 * (1 + .01)^1 = \$50.50.$$

Imagine you are holding GameStop stock indefinitely and you want to know its present value. Over long holding periods, changes in the market price of the share become insignificant. The present value therefore depends largely on the earnings growth rate. To find the present value, add the present discounted value of each dividend payment for each subsequent year——which becomes tedious——or use the *earnings discount model*, which extends the logic of earnings growth rates mentioned above. This model suggests that the present value of an indefinite series of earnings is the same as the present value of a Consol—a bond that offers a payment for an infinite number of years: $P_t = \dfrac{D * (1 + g)}{(i - g)}$. For example, if you expect GameStop has a dividend growth rate of 1 percent, dividend payments equal to $50, and an annual interest rate of 5 percent, its present value equals

$$P_0 = \frac{\$50(1 + 0.01)}{0.05 - 0.01} = \$1,262.50.$$

The general lesson is that stock prices depend on a person's expectations about a firm's profitability. Thus, higher D's (earnings) and g's (earnings growth rates) lead to higher present values and higher stock prices.

Stocks Are Better in Markets, From Coffeehouses to Skyscrapers

Stock markets emerge whenever people who are willing to sell stocks transact with people who are willing to purchase stocks. When many investors want to buy and sell shares, stock exchanges arise to efficiently match buyers with sellers.

The United States has the largest stock market with the New York Stock Exchange (NYSE)—with a market capitalization of approximately $26 trillion worth of outstanding stocks. The NYSE was one of the scores of securities exchanges to form in the United States after 1790 and was second to Philadelphia's exchange until after the War of 1812. Over time, many smaller exchanges closed as new technologies, like telegraphic and telephonic systems, made it easier to trade in larger, though more distant, exchanges that provided investors with more liquidity, in other words, the ability to buy or sell shares faster and/or for less money.

China's stock exchanges have grown along with that nation's economy. The Shanghai Stock Exchange (SSE)——recently the third largest in the world with a market capitalization of over $7.6 trillion——began in the mid-19th century. By 1930, it facilitated exchanges between Chinese and foreign investors, but Japanese occupation halted its operations during the Second World War. In 1949, China's new Communist government forced it to close until reforms in 1990.

The Shenzhen Stock Exchange (SZSE), the world's ninth largest stock market, has a market capitalization of approximately $2.5 trillion. Formed in 1990 as a part of China's economic liberalization, the SZSE quickly attracted investors from nearby Hong Kong and abroad. The Shenzhen special economic zone's relatively free economic policies encouraged population growth and rising wealth, further bolstering the SZSE.

Regardless of locale, stock markets allow myriad individuals to assess company prospects. The better those expectations are, the more people are willing to pay for its shares. The worse those expectations are, the less people are willing to pay. While the price of shares in the secondary market (stock markets), as opposed to primary (issuance) markets, do not directly affect corporations, declining share prices serve as a warning that outsiders (investors) see trouble looming.

Figure 6.2 shows one example where positive expectations of profit lead to higher share prices. On January 13, 2020, Moderna finalized the mRNA-1273 sequence for what would become the Moderna COVID-19 vaccine. Months before the initial outbreaks of COVID-19 in the United States—in March 2020—and long before the CDC recommended the vaccine's use in adults on December 19, 2020, investors believed Moderna stock was undervalued, so they began buying it, which bid up its price.

Changsheng Bio Technology, the second largest Chinese manufacturer of rabies and chickenpox vaccines in 2017, contrasts with the success of Moderna. In July 2018, the Chinese State Drug Administration accused Changsheng of breaking vaccine laws and protocols based on a series of inspections and whistleblower reports. Ultimately, Changsheng had been

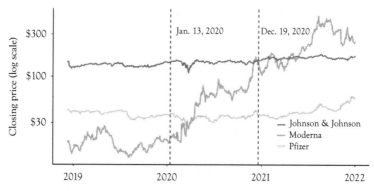

Figure 6.2 Vaccine makers, 2018 to 2022

Source: Yahoo Finance using quantmod R package.

selling ineffective rabies and DPT vaccines. Whereas Changsheng share price averaged approximately ¥24 (yuan) in June and early July of 2018, it fell precipitously on July 13 and trended toward ¥0 throughout the summer and fall of 2018.

Economists formulated the *efficient markets hypothesis*, which predicts that stock prices reflect the underlying value of a firm given all available information. Investors can profit by buying a share if they believe a corporation's stock is undervalued, or selling it if they believe the stock is over-valued. Competition drives individuals to improve their expectations and adjust their decisions. Thus, we should expect stock prices to reflect rational expectations—not wishful thinking—about corporate profitability. The implications of this hypothesis are profound.

Information Spreads Fast in Stock Markets

Driven by competition, investors create effective information feedback loops. That is, they base decisions to buy or sell on expectations of future value and available information. Investors who tend to form more accurate expectations are rewarded with investment gains, whereas those who tend to form less accurate expectations are punished with losses.

The Chernobyl nuclear power plant disaster of 1986 provides one example of how quickly efficient markets react to new information. As one of the Chernobyl nuclear power plants exploded on April 26, 1986—and continued to leak radiation for the next nine days—radiation spread throughout the region and into the Ukraine region of the Soviet Union, potentially contaminating wheat and potato crops.

As one might expect, commodity prices increased throughout the area but also in the United States. Here is a report from *The Los Angeles Times* on May 1, 1986:

> U.S. farm commodity prices rose sharply for the second straight day Wednesday amid speculation that a possible meltdown at a second Soviet nuclear reactor in Chernobyl increases the potential for damage to that nation's grain and livestock production, and for bigger sales of U.S. food overseas (Sing 1986).

Within minutes upon hearing reports of disaster, commodities speculators had driven up the prices of agricultural staples, while investors bought or sold the stocks of food processors and retailers, like supermarket chains, depending on how they believed higher food prices would affect profits. Astute investors also bought shares in banks that lent to farmers, who were less likely to default due to the windfall.

The tragic events surrounding the space shuttle Challenger, which exploded at 11:39 am EST on January 28, 1986, provide an even richer example of the efficient markets hypothesis. As Maloney and Mulherin (2003) explain, three interesting things occurred immediately after the explosion.

First, stock prices for the corporations that built the shuttle fell. Within 21 minutes of the explosion and 13 minutes of the News Wire account, Lockheed, Martin Marietta (external fuel tank manufacturers), and Rockwell (manufacturer of the shuttle and its engines) were down 5.05, 2.83, and 6.12 percent, respectively.

Second, stock prices for the corporation that made the defective O-ring part, Morton Thiokol, experienced particular and sustained declines, which reflects a significant loss in expected future value. Morton Thiokol's stock was the only one to experience a temporary trading halt—issued by the NYSE—and a continual decline on January 28. Morton Thiokol stock prices fell by 6.06 percent during the trading halt and fell an additional 1.79 percent by 1 pm. Furthermore, whereas prices for other aerospace firms recovered, Morton Thiokol prices reflected the shock of January 28 at least until April.

Third, and perhaps most importantly, stock prices reacted two weeks before acclaimed physicist Richard Feynman publicly demonstrated for the first time how shuttle O-rings became defective. The Rogers Commission investigating the explosion did not officially blame Morton Thiokol's O-rings until June. Maloney and Mulherin (2003, 457) states that

> The fact that market liquidity was available to maintain a market in Lockheed, Martin Marietta, and Rockwell while the market for Morton Thiokol dried up suggests that the stock market discerned the guilty party within minutes of the announcement of the crash.

Likely, insiders knew O-rings were to blame and transmitted the information by selling off Morton Thiokol stock.

And Faster Still With Online and Handheld Markets

In 1790, it took an entire day to travel between the stock markets of New York and Philadelphia. If one wanted to engage in arbitrage (riskless trade) by buying low in one city and selling high in the other before the market prices synced back up, one needed a fast horse or a faster way of communicating the price discrepancy, which was done using a semaphoric system of flags in day and fires at night. Later, telegraphic systems proved even faster and cheaper. Financial systems have always spurred information innovation.

Moreover, we should expect price differences to fall as transaction costs fall. The advent of wired communications in the 1830s, for example, decreased communication costs and gave people more opportunities to exploit price differences—within minutes rather than hours by semaphore or days by horse. Price *tickers* became more common by the 1850s and continued to become specialized. The advent of fiber optic cables linked to computerized trading algorithms has whittled this time to nanoseconds.

Internet and phone-based trading platforms like E-Trade and Robinhood have lowered the transaction costs of investing, which, like trade execution times, have been trending lower over time. Faster, cheaper trading increases the number of investors, the number of trades, and the efficiency of markets.

Don't Expect to Beat the Market

Markets foster competition, and prices reflect underlying values, so don't expect to make long-term profits by actively buying and selling stocks. Efficient markets theory suggests profit opportunities exist, but they quickly disappear as other investors bid prices up, or down. Even investors who possess inside (nonpublic) information or uncommon insight will see prices move toward fair value as others mimic their success.

The point is not that investors should eschew the stock market, it is that a profit-maximizing strategy rarely includes actively buying and selling stocks. To make the active strategy work consistently, investors must produce novel and accurate analyses that consistently produce information about which stock prices will rise and fall and trade so as to earn more money than the analyses cost to produce. Remember that costs refer to opportunity costs; the dollars and time people spend on market research have alternative uses. It is not clear anyone has such abilities, and if anyone does, he, she, or it has strong incentives to hide that fact. It appears that the benefits of actively managing a portfolio are not clearly better than putting funds into a diversified portfolio of stocks—like an indexed mutual fund—that passively tracks the market growth rate. When stocks are diversified, moreover, volatility falls without reducing average returns. Indeed, most investors today invest in passive funds with low fees (Malkiel 2019). One of the first studies on this, the Cowles Commission report, compared the performance of expert stock picks—from surveys of fire insurance managers, other financiers, and financial reporters—with a random selection (Cowles 1933). The report found the experts performed worse.

Seriously, Everyone Thinks They Are Smarter

Wealthy investors balk at such claims. Their wealth, they suggest, indicates the fallibility of the efficient markets hypothesis. It does not. We aren't saying it is impossible to earn profit from buying low and selling high. We are saying that it is highly unlikely for anyone to consistently beat the market, and such success might be attributable solely to luck. A broken (analog) clock is right twice a day; similarly, a person might flip a coin 50 times and get all heads. Attributing that outcome—which is purely a matter of probability—to anything more than random chance, for example, the skill or intellect of the coin flipper, seems unwarranted. Similarly, successful investors might have randomly picked consistent winners.

You might still think you can beat the market. If so, consider (1) the publicness of what you think you know and (2) why others are not prohibited from taking advantage of the same situation. People who actively buy/sell think they have relatively novel and relevant information, and that there are large costs to others of acquiring that information. They could be correct. Proponents of the efficient market hypothesis, however, argue that it is highly likely that other people know what you know because communication and information costs are low.

Ultimately, investors can follow or disregard the logic of competitive markets it they wish. Most observations about stock markets, however, support the efficient market hypothesis, and hence the superiority of low cost, indexed mutual funds.

CHAPTER 7

Derivatives

Derivatives are contracts that *derive* their value from another financial instrument or other underlying assets. Whereas houses are assets whose value is derived from its use to homeowners, houses are not derivatives as they are not financial instruments. Stocks are a type of financial instrument, but they derive their value from the underlying profitability of a firm—rather than another financial instrument—and are not generally considered to be derivatives. Forward contracts, however, are derivatives as they are promises to exchange goods in the future at prices determined today.

Derivatives are neither good nor bad, they are tools. They mitigate or transfer risk, and they facilitate economic calculation. Once again, financial innovations make people better off.

College Students Are Forward-Thinking

People often buy goods with the intention of consuming shortly after purchase. People also buy goods with the intention of delaying consumption. Consider the problems graduating seniors at Randolph University might face. They want to throw an end-of-the-year celebration with lots of beer. They collected $1,000, but they don't want to buy beer when prices might be lowest, say three months before the party. If they purchased beer, then they would be tempted to have smaller parties before the big one, and the beer would probably go bad before the party. They could purchase the beer a couple hours before the party, but they are exposed to the risk of varying prices. This could mean the difference between a regular party—with 40 24 packs (at $25 per pack)—and the best party ever—with 50 24 packs (at $20 per pack).

The beer distributor faces a related problem: she wants to maximize net revenue by selling beer, but she does not know how much people will buy. Net revenue will inevitably fall the more she over- or underestimates this number. Moreover, she is likely in a competitive market where total revenue depends on retail market prices, which could rise or fall. If the retail price of a 24 pack fell from $25 to $20 while the wholesale cost stayed the same, her profits would suffer.

If the Randolph students and the beer distributor realize their problems are related, they will agree to buy and sell beer in the future but at current prices. The students are better off because they locked in a relatively low price and will receive the beer in the future, when they want it, and the distributor is better off because she knows what to expect. In doing this, they create a financial instrument known as a *forward contract*, which mitigates the risks each party faces regarding price fluctuations. Such contracts are an agreement to exchange goods in the future but at current prices.

So Are Farmers and Airline Executives

Farmers have used forward contracts for centuries to avoid the risks associated with drought, disease and pestilence, bumper crop conditions, and myriad other factors that influence crop prices. As commodities' prices fluctuate, farmers bear risk as they endeavor to bring crops to the market. They could acquire planting equipment and seeds, hire workers, sow and tend the fields for months to what end? They could face a situation— months or years after they initiated the process—where the price per unit is $100 or $10, depending on the prevailing conditions of supply and demand. Forward contracts improve expectations about the monetary reward of farming by locking in prices today.

Airline managers face a similar problem with the price of aviation fuel. They want to maximize net revenue, but the price of aviation fuel could be $80 per barrel, or it could be $100 per barrel. For however many flights they offer, the price of aviation fuel could mean they earn positive or negative net revenue. Thus, they want to lock in the price of aviation fuel today and receive it at a later date, when needed. Aviation fuel producers are better off too as they now know how much oil they should process and how many barrels people might want. Forward contracts encourage long-term planning.

Forwards Are Contracts and Costly

Like all contracts, though, forward contracts are costly to write. Finding a counterparty, a person willing to agree to your terms, might be difficult. Randolph seniors might spend hours or days finding a willing distributor, if they find one at all. Airline executives might use up a lot of aviation fuel finding an aviation fuel producer willing to lock in a fuel price.

Another problem people face when making forward contracts is that typically one of the parties will face an incentive to renege after the contract is signed. Consider a forward contract—between an airline executive and an aviation fuel refinery—that requires the delivery of 1,000 barrels of jet fuel in three months at a price of $80 per barrel.

Say that the price of fuel rises to $85 per barrel in three months. Abiding by the terms of the contract means that the seller must sell at a price that is $5 lower than the prevailing market price. The seller must sell each barrel at $15 below the prevailing market price when that price is $100. The seller faces an incentive to renege whenever someone is willing to purchase fuel at a price above the price stipulated in the forward contract.

Say the market price of fuel falls to $75 per barrel at the end of three months. Abiding by the terms of the contract means the airline must pay $5 above the prevailing market price for each barrel. And they would pay an additional $20 per barrel if the market price decreased to $60. The executive faces an incentive to renege whenever someone is willing to sell fuel at a price below the price stipulated in the forward contract.

Repeated dealings and other contracting mechanisms, that is, leases and vertical integration, might lower transaction costs and resolve the risks people face. People enter into lease and rental agreements that, in effect, lock-in prices and deliver goods at a future date. An apartment lease, for example, bundles multiple forward contracts, which facilitates exchange between apartment owners and renters and encourages long-term planning. To avoid the risks associated with price fluctuations, firms might engage in vertical integration—instead of or in addition to using forward contracts. That is, a firm might purchase another firm that produces a relevant input. For example, Delta airlines recently purchased a refinery to avoid price fluctuations in aviation fuel—an input that comprised about 30 percent of its total costs (Almansur, Megginson, and Pugachev 2020).[1]

Futures Are More General

The transaction costs of writing forward contracts fall with the advent of futures contracts, clearinghouses, and futures markets. A futures contract is a standardized forward contract that is easily transferable and often exchanged through an organized market. Consider the jet fuel forward from before. One of the features that turns that forward into a futures contract is that many people can buy and sell it; moreover, it can be written again. Futures contracts are more widely used than forward contracts.

Organized futures markets and clearinghouses lower the transaction costs for futures in significant ways. Clearinghouses emerged to lower transaction costs and minimize risks as financial markets became larger and more sophisticated in the United States during the 19th century. In particular, clearinghouses guarantee payment if either party fails to follow the terms of a futures contract. In exchange for taking on these risks, clearinghouses also require both parties to deposit funds in a *margin account*.

When futures contracts are purchased and sold in futures markets or clearinghouses—like the Chicago Mercantile Exchange, the National Stock Exchange of India, and EUREX in Germany—buyers and sellers become easier to find, contracts become standardized and more enforceable, weights and measurements become more uniform, and transportation services become easier to arrange.

As more buyers and sellers interact in futures markets, the more futures prices converge, and the more people engage in economic calculation. Recalling our discussion on efficient markets from Chapter 7, one of the key markers of an efficient futures market is that the price of futures contracts tends to equal the price of the underlying asset or commodity.

---

[1] Almansur, Megginson, and Pugachev (2020) note that while the mere ownership of a refinery does not reduce price fluctuations in crude oil, it does reduce the difference between the price of jet fuel and crude oil, which influences the airline's bottom line.

Note that as a futures contract expires a profit opportunity would exist if a price differential between the contract and the underlying asset persisted. Because people readily exploit such profit opportunities, price differences tend to disappear.

Consider a futures contract that promises delivery of 1,000 barrels of fuel in three months at a market price of $80. Minutes before the futures contract expires, however, say that the market price of fuel is $70. Anyone could purchase fuel at $70, sell fuel futures for $80, and agree to deliver the fuel shortly.[2] This arbitrage opportunity would net $10 per transaction.

The more people exploit the opportunity to earn $10—with negligible risk—the smaller the price difference becomes. This difference shrinks because more people will purchase fuel—to take advantage of the different prices—but this tends to increase the demand for fuel and its price. At the same time, the price of fuel futures will fall as more and more people are willing to provide them. Importantly, this logic applies throughout the length of the futures contract, which suggests that we should expect to see the price of a futures contract align with the underlying commodity or asset after the future contracts is signed and before its expiration date.

Options and Swaps Transfer Risk Too

Options are another kind of derivative that gives people a right but not an obligation to purchase (call) or sell (put) an asset at a predetermined price on (European) or before (American) a specified date. These derivatives are useful when people face periods of uncertainty. Imagine a small town that might want to provide snow plowing in the winter or tree removal after an unusually severe storm. Or imagine a sudden heat wave increases the demand for AC and increases the price of electricity. These events are costly, but options provide a kind of insurance by giving the holder of a call (put) the right to purchase (sell) services at a predetermined price.

---

[2] You might already have the fuel futures or you might borrow them, which could still be profitable.

Consider options on Boeing stock. Purchasing a July 2030 call for 1,000 shares at $250—known as the strike price—gives the owner the right to purchase Boeing at $250 before July 2030 regardless of the prevailing market price. Purchasing a July 2030 put for 1,000 shares at the same strike price gives the owner the right to sell those shares at $250 before July 2030 regardless of the prevailing market price. Sellers of those options receive a premium in exchange for obligating themselves to sell or buy shares when the option owner exercises the call or put, respectively.

Options are an innovative kind of insurance or hedge. Notice that buying a call allows people to minimize the costs associated with purchasing assets at higher prices; similarly, buying a put allows people to minimize the costs associated with selling assets at lower prices. Options allow option sellers to assume risks in exchange for the premium revenue from *writing* the options. At the same time, options might not ever be *in the money* and hence might never be exercised.

Moreover, options encourage speculation, which helps people to clarify their expectations about future prices. Some people expect the share price of Boeing will rise; purchasing a call option rewards those expectations once the market price exceeds the strike price. The option holder can then exercise the call, obtain Boeing at the strike price, and sell the shares at market, pocketing the difference. Some people expect the share price of Boeing will fall; purchasing a put option rewards those expectations once the market price sinks below the strike price. The option holder can then buy Boeing low in the market and sell it at the higher strike price and pocket the difference. As market activity plays out, the option holder might be right or wrong. Worst-case scenario, the option holder loses the price of the option. Best-case scenario is that the option holder is rewarded for their relatively accurate expectations with a wide margin between the strike and market prices.

As options become more widely traded, we should expect market prices to form. Consistent with the logic of supply and demand described in Chapter 4, options prices rise under the following conditions. As the strike price rises, the value of a call decreases, and the value of a put increases. As the price of the underlying asset rises, the value of a call will rise, and the value of a put will fall. As the length of time between expiration and exercising an option rises, calls and puts rise in value. Similarly,

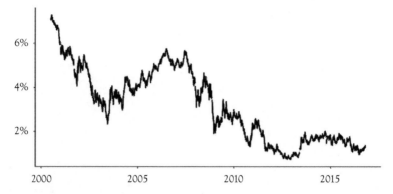

Figure 7.1 The daily five-year swap rate, 2000 to 2016

Source: FRED database using fredr.

as volatility in the price of the underlying asset rises, the value of calls and puts rise.

Swaps—on interest rates, share prices, foreign exchange rates—are another kind of derivative whereby market participants make periodic exchanges based on the nominal value of an asset. With interest rate swaps, one side of the exchange makes payments based on a fixed interest rate, while the other side makes payments based on a variable interest rate. With credit default swaps, one side of the exchange makes regular cash payments, while the other side makes payments in the event of default. Figure 7.1 shows the Intercontinental Exchange (ICE) five-year swap rate, which is a commonly used benchmark used to write swap contracts.[3]

More than a source of speculation, swaps help participants to share risk. They allow lenders like banks to make loans without bearing the consequences of default. By using interest rate swaps, banks can reduce interest rate risk, that is, the risk associated with changing interest rates. Banks experience this risk as they make long-term loans like mortgages—often at fixed interest rates—and have short-term obligations like checking accounts—at variable interest rates.

---

[3] This is the mid-price for interest-rate swaps—that range from 1 to 30 years—denominated in euros, U.S. dollars, and in British pounds.

Derivatives Add Stability and Risk
to Financial Markets

Derivative contracts help smooth prices and transfer risk, which helps explain the growth in derivatives markets since 1970. During the last three decades of the 20th century, derivatives markets grew as interest rates and exchange rates experienced large changes, as transaction costs fell with advances in computing and communications technology, and as people acquired sophisticated means of evaluating derivatives, for example, the Black–Scholes model (Stulz 2004). The Bank of International Settlement reports that the notional value of all contracts in the global derivatives market was approximately $606 trillion in 2020. While that impressive sum sounds like more than global GDP, it merely represents the sums of the underlying assets, not the sums at risk. For example, a swap whereby two banks agreed to swap $1 million per year in exchange for $900,000 plus a variable interest rate annually for a decade would have a notional value of some $20 million even though the net annual payments might never exceed a few thousand dollars.

Moreover, derivatives are particularly important means of transferring risk for individuals and nonfinancial firms. Relative to larger, more established financial firms, individuals and nonfinancial firms face higher costs associated with acquiring alternative means of transferring risk. The more people can put themselves in positions to manage risk via derivative contracts, the more they are able to engage in productive projects, which increases their productivity and wealth.

At the same time, derivatives come with their own risks. While forward, futures, and basic options contracts can be evaluated with relative ease—aided by relatively thick markets where prices adequately reflect the value of the derivative—more complicated derivatives are not as liquid. In the early 1990s, for example, Gibson Greetings and Bankers Trust wrote the following swap: Gibson would pay Bankers Trust $\dfrac{LIBOR^2}{.06} * \$30,000,000$, and Bankers Trust would pay $0.055 * \$30,000,000$ (Hansell 1994; Stulz 2004). Gibson Greetings eventually sued Bankers Trust for fraud and deception—as the six-month LIBOR rate began to rise, the payments going to Bankers Trust became larger than the payments going to Gibson Greetings. It seems, however, that Gibson Greetings should have paid more attention to how changes in the LIBOR rate influenced the value of the swap.[4]

In any event, relatively complicated derivatives are less liquid as people might be less willing to purchase them. As the market for such derivatives is relatively thin or weaker, there is a greater chance that prices do not adequately reflect the rational value of the derivative. The more prices fail to reflect the underlying value of derivative contracts, the greater default risks counterparties face. That is, individuals will revise their balance sheets (upward or downward) when they realize the value of their derivative contracts. Such risks might become a source of instability throughout financial markets, especially if financial intermediaries are selling or are exposed to complex derivatives. As helpful as derivatives can be, they might discourage financial transactions with any individuals and firms with large holdings of complicated derivatives as assets.

A Short Story About Short Selling, Short Squeezing, GameStop, and Robinhood

With our understanding of stock markets and derivatives markets, we can now understand why there was so much price volatility and controversy surrounding GameStop, Robinhood, AMC, Hertz, and other equities in January and February 2021. Each story has multiple layers as financial instruments are complex, and individuals face myriad decisions.

Let's focus on GameStop stock to clarify. Whereas Figure 6.1 shows the change in GME from 2011, Figure 7.2 shows the change in GME from January 1 to April 1, 2021.

Understanding the GME saga begins with the recognition that the price of GME had been on a downward trend since 2016. To many analysts and investors, this trend presented a profit opportunity via short selling. Short sellers borrow shares they believe are overvalued and sell them with the expectation that they will decline in price. They can then buy the shares back at a lower price, return the borrowed shares, and

---

[4] Bankers Trust settled with Gibson Greetings in 1994.

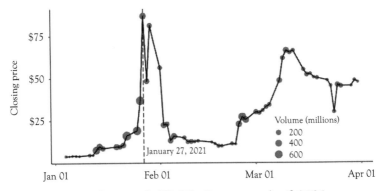

Figure 7.2 *GameStop stock (GME), January to April 2021*

Source: Yahoo Finance using quantmod R package.

keep the difference. For example, if I borrow 1,000 shares of GME and immediately sell them at a prevailing price of $20, I have $20,000. If the price of GME were to fall to $10, I spend $10,000 to purchase 1,000 shares and return them to the lender leaving me with $10,000 (minus the borrowing fee). Shorting GME was—and still is—a widespread practice; an average of 90 percent of the outstanding GME shares had been sold short in 2020.

In mid-January, 2021, flash mob investors—organized through social media and Reddit—learned more about this profit opportunity, and discovered one of their own. Moreover, they explicitly wanted to best sophisticated Wall Street traders. They expected that if the price of GME increased—driven by their enthusiasm and interest in GME and their efforts to bolster its price—they could go long, or buy low now and sell high later.

Moreover, investors who had been shorting GME were in a bind; rising GME prices meant less—potentially negative—net revenue. If I borrowed 1,000 shares and sold them when GME was $20, I have $20,000; if the price of GME rises to $21—and my shares are due—I am obligated to pay $21,000 to return the shares. I've lost $1,000. To cover these loses, or at least minimize the damage, investors who had been shorting GME rushed to purchase at relatively low but rising prices. The increased demand for GME—from people covering their short positions and from people going long—pushed GME prices higher throughout January.

On January 11, GME was approaching $20, but it peaked at $347.51 on January 27.

Many investors and hedge funds who had been shorting GME were able to cover the rising prices, and those who were not went bankrupt. Estimates of the losses range from $5 to $12 billion.

Another layer to this story concerns Robinhood and its controversial decision to halt trading on its app of particular stocks like GME. Robinhood is a smartphone-based equities and assets trading application with no commission fees that provides a significant reduction in the transaction costs associated with buying and selling stocks, for example, searching for interested buyers and sellers and managing counterparty risk (for more on technology, the sharing economy, and transaction costs, see Munger 2018). Spurred by news of the GME short selling and startled Wall Street investors, hundreds of thousands of customers created Robinhood accounts in January to pursue what they perceived as potential profit opportunities.

Like other stockbrokers, Robinhood reduces transaction costs by using a clearinghouse to manage counterparty risk. Prior to finalizing a trade, the clearinghouse ensures both parties have the requisite funds to make the exchange. This clearance and settlement process takes two days—as ruled by the Securities Exchange Commission—and until the process is complete, brokers must provide a percentage of each trade as collateral. As hundreds of thousands of users began to trade GME—and other stocks—Robinhood's clearinghouse required them to post more collateral, about $3 billion. While Robinhood met initial requests, its managers quickly became concerned about finding the requisite funds if the current level of trading activity continued for the foreseeable future. To reduce the amount required by the clearinghouse, Robinhood temporarily halted trading on GME and other hot stocks on January 27 and 28.

Headlines soon told stories of people who tried to buy or sell GME but were locked out. People were quick to blame Robinhood or claim they were working with Wall Street insiders to foreclose equities markets to small-time investors. Yet, its actions constituted a prudent response to increased volatility.

We should also recognize the role loose fiscal and monetary policies played—topics we will discuss further in later chapters. Providing people with additional cash balances might be an appropriate response to alleviate the shock of a pandemic; however, it left many with additional funds. Perhaps people would have been more cautious if they had been spending their own dollars. We also wonder whether investors who fared worse could have spent more time conducting their own analysis. That is, it seems unfair to claim there are inherent problems with Robinhood, with equities markets, and with capitalism when more prudent investors exercised caution.

Lastly, GME represents another story about the efficiency of equities markets. That is, while the price of GME had been declining since 2016, it has oscillated above $150 since early 2021. This suggests something more than the temporary effect of Redditors. Perhaps people believe the stock was initially undervalued. Perhaps people recognize that the GameStop of 2021 has improved upon the GameStop of previous years.

CHAPTER 8

Foreign Exchange

People buy most goods with their domestic currency, but sometimes a seller from another currency area wants payment in their domestic currency, not that of the buyer. German automobile manufacturers, for example, need to pay their workers in euros, so they might want to be paid in euros even if the buyer is an American accustomed to transacting in dollars. Here again, the financial system helps to facilitate real-world trade via intermediaries and markets. Foreign exchange markets allow for the exchange of currencies that have different, and often rapidly fluctuating, values.

A Market Like Any Other

Foreign trade implies a market for foreign currency. Trillions of U.S. dollars worth of currencies are traded daily, more than any other market. If economic entities in the United States want to buy German goods, economic entities that hold euros must be willing to buy dollars and sell euros. Figure 8.1 shows the U.S.-euro exchange rate since the euro's creation in 1998.

The nominal exchange rate indicates how much one currency is worth relative to another, and *vice versa*. For example, if the exchange rate between the United States and Europe is $2 per €1, the reciprocal is also true, that is, €0.50 purchases $1.

Changes in exchange rates indicate changes in the value of one currency relative to another. Whereas the dollar–euro exchange rate, $E_{\$/\unicode{x20AC}}$ was 1.17 in October 2020, it was 1.16 in October 2021. That decline in the nominal exchange rate indicates that euros became worth less and dollars worth more relative to each other. That is, €1 purchased fewer dollars in 2021 than it did in 2020. Whenever a currency falls in value relative to another currency, it is said to weaken or depreciate; whenever a currency

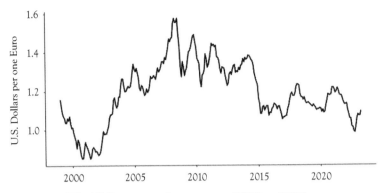

Figure 8.1 The U.S.-euro exchange rate, 1999 to 2023

Source: FRED database using fredr.

rises in value relative to another currency, it is said to strengthen or appreciate. Currencies are not properly said to be *strong* or *weak*, just stronger or weaker in relation to another currency and over some time span.

There's Nothing Immoral or Unpatriotic About Importing and Exporting

The more you look at Figure 8.1 the more you might notice that since 2008, the U.S.-euro exchange rate has declined, meaning the dollar has strengthened or appreciated against the euro because fewer dollars are needed to purchase a euro. Does this mean one area is better than the other? Consider the following quotes:

- "Strong dollars are overall very good." (Donald Trump)
- "As your President, one would think that I would be thrilled with our very strong dollar. I am not!" (Donald Trump)
- "One of the most important factors in our trade deficit and our weak export levels is the value of our currency…We should consider a number of tools…to produce a currency value that's better for our workers and our industries." (Team Warren)

Politicians want strong and weak currency depending on whichever one serves their interests, but we shouldn't let the descriptors of weak and strong distract us from the meaning behind exchange rates. Exchange rates merely indicate changes in the purchasing power of one currency relative to another. As U.S. dollars appreciate relative to euros, dollars can buy more euros, which makes European goods seem cheaper than similar goods in the United States. Thus, when a currency appreciates, imports tend to increase; when a currency depreciates, exports tend to increase.

Such changes are neither good nor bad overall; however, they can make some people worse off and some people better off. As the dollar-euro exchange rate rises, for example, dollars depreciate. That is, it now takes more dollars to purchase one euro. People in the United States are going to export more goods to people in Europe; thus, individuals and firms who make goods that will be exported are better off. People who had previously imported goods from Europe, however, are worse off because they need to use more dollars to buy the necessary number of euros.

Supply and Demand Still Hold

We see constant short-run fluctuations in nominal exchange rates. Supply and demand explain much of this variation. In the following discussion, U.S. dollar (USD) is the domestic currency.

The Supply of Dollars

The supply of dollars (USD) comes from people who have dollars, they want to sell them, and they want to purchase foreign goods or assets. If you study abroad in France, if you purchase Honda shares, or if you invest in Eurobonds, you will be a supplier of dollars. To purchase goods while you are abroad, you can't use dollars, so you will sell them. Similarly, if you are buying Honda shares or buying Eurobonds, you will have to sell dollars. Just like other supply curves, the quantity of dollars people are willing to give rises with the price, which in this case is the exchange rate. If dollars are worth more in terms of foreign currency, you will be more willing to sell dollars.

Changes in the supply schedule of dollars occur for many reasons. For example, if people want to buy more domestic goods, they won't want to sell their dollars as much. The supply of dollars would fall, which tends to raise the exchange rate and strengthen the dollar. But if people developed a greater appreciation for Chinese goods, for example, the supply of dollars would rise, which tends to lower the exchange rate and weaken the dollar.

Changes in the relative return of foreign assets also influences the foreign exchange market. That is, whenever a foreign asset has a higher return, relative to a comparable asset in the United States, people will want to purchase the foreign asset. This means they will be more willing to sell their dollars. Thus, we should expect a fall in the exchange rate as foreign assets become more attractive relative to domestic assets. For example, if the real interest rate on foreign bonds rises relative to U.S. bonds, those bonds become more valuable. Similarly, if foreign assets become less risky, people will want to hold them rather than U.S. assets, all else equal. Thus, we should expect the supply of dollars to rise when foreign assets become less risky.

Finally, the supply of dollars might change as people change their expectations about the future value of dollars. If people expect the value of a dollar will fall in the future, they can purchase more foreign goods today—while the exchange rate is relatively high. As people develop expectations of a higher rate of inflation, for example, the expected future value of dollars falls, which increases the current supply of dollars and lowers the exchange rate.

The Demand for Dollars

The demand for dollars comes from people who want to buy dollars to purchase American goods or assets. This symmetry between who supplies dollars and who demands them suggests we can dispense with an exhaustive list of the factors that influencing demand. That is, whereas people in the United States supply dollars to acquire foreign goods and assets, people abroad demand dollars to acquire American goods and assets. This means that the factors that influence demand are the same as the factors that influence supply, though from the perspective of foreigners.

Long-Run Changes

To explain long-run movements in exchange rates—changes over years and decades, as in Figure 8.1—note that the local prices of goods adjust based on local market changes. The implication of long-run price flexibility is that the prices of goods tend to equalize across borders. That is, we should observe similar prices for similar goods in different places, accounting for transaction costs. For example, if the dollar price of a Porsche is $100,000 in the United States, but it is $70,000 in Germany, we would expect that entrepreneurs will take advantage of this price difference by buying cars in Germany, shipping them to the United States, and selling them there, until the prices are equalized in the two markets, net of shipping and other costs.[1]

The notion that prices of identical goods should be identical, net of transaction costs, is called the Law of One Price when applied to one good and purchasing power parity (PPP) when applied economywide. More generally, this means that the real exchange rate, the dollar value of a good or a basket of goods in the United States relative to the dollar value of the same good or basket of goods abroad tends toward equality. Thus, PPP implies that the relative rate of inflation is an important driver of long-run changes in exchange rates. A high rate of inflation in Country A relative to that in Country B should depreciate the currency of A relative to B. As the United States tends to have higher inflation than the Euro Zone, for example, dollars tend to depreciate relative to the euro, all else equal.

A Nominal and Real Affair

The nominal exchange rates discussed are the rates at which people exchange two currencies. Economic entities, however, want to know whether they will have more of a good if they purchase locally or abroad. To determine that, they want to know the *real* exchange rate, which accounts for the price of a good in both locations at the prevailing nominal exchange rate. Generally, the real exchange rate, from the perspective of an American, is the dollar price of a domestic good divided by the

---

[1] There might be minor differences between these cars, for example, the steering wheel might be on the *wrong* side, but we wouldn't expect this to deter such strong profit opportunities. At least driving a right-handed car is, generally, legal in the United States.

dollar price of a foreign good. For example, if the same beer is $5 per pint in Richmond, Virginia, 30 pesos per pint in Mexico City, and the nominal exchange rate is $0.049 per 1 peso, the real beer exchange rate is:

$$\frac{Dollar\ price\ of\ beer\ in\ Richmond}{Peso\ price\ of\ beer\ in\ Mexico\ City * E_{dollar/peso}}$$

So:

$$\frac{\$5}{30\ pesos * \$0.049\ /\ 1\ peso} = \frac{\$5}{\$1.47} = 3.40$$

The real beer exchange rate between Richmond and Mexico City indicates that one beer in Richmond is worth almost three and a half in Mexico City, given the prevailing prices, the nominal exchange rate, and all other supply and demand conditions remained the same.

Again, this assumes that the beer in Richmond is the same as the beer in Mexico City (and that a pint is the same size in both places). This might be true for some brand name beer, but not for others. Differences in these kinds of goods suggest different markets and different prices, even if we accounted for the exchange rate. The real beer exchange rate allows us to compare the value of currencies when we are looking at similar beer. Also, the equalization of prices net of transaction costs holds only for goods that can be traded internationally. Some goods, like

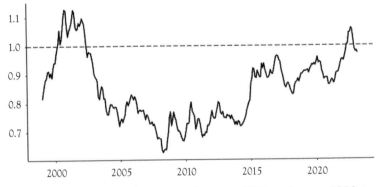

Figure 8.2 The real exchange rate between USD and euro, 1999 to 2023

Source: FRED database using fredr.

getting a haircut and buying unique parcels of land, cannot be traded due to their nature, while others face legal restrictions and taxes.

One can use the preceding formula to compute a real exchange rate for the entire internationally traded portion of the economy using the appropriate consumer price index, as in Figure 8.2.

Interpreting Figure 8.2 is similar to the example of the real beer exchange rate. Whenever the real exchange rate is greater than 1, foreign goods seem cheaper. Figure 8.2 shows the real exchange rate between the USD and the euro area has been consistently below 1 since 2003, which suggests that European goods seem more expensive than U.S. goods to people in the United States. Generally, this exchange rate favors American exporters.

CHAPTER 9

Competition and Financial Intermediaries

We now have a better understanding of how financial markets work. We should also recognize that competition within these markets encourages suppliers of financial goods to discover better ways of making their customers happy. An important way in which markets encourage people to organize financial services is through the creation of financial intermediaries like commercial and investment banks, insurance companies, and pension funds. In competitive settings, financial intermediaries face incentives to find better, cheaper ways of providing credit and liquidity, developing insurance plans, and offering various kinds of investment opportunities, for example, pension plans. Competition between stock exchanges, covered in Chapter 6, also creates incentives to resolve problems related to information asymmetry, which refers to differences in the kind of information people have about the quality of goods and/or the trustworthiness of a partner. Asymmetric information is the most pernicious problem facing financial market participants, but competitive financial intermediaries manage it in the most efficient ways technologically possible.

Financial Intermediaries Are Matchmakers

There are good reasons you don't buy stocks at the grocery store or don't offer to make loans at your local gas station. The transaction costs associated with making those kinds of exchanges are too high in those places. If you were interested in buying stocks at such places, could you trust the cashier? Perhaps, but unlike apples or steaks, the value of a stock is not easily assessed and transferable over the counter. Even today, stocks mostly take only electronic form and are deliverable a few days in the future. It is not clear your average cashier could facilitate such transactions. Would you earn positive profits by lending cash to strangers at the gas station? By finding ways to bond transactions, especially between strangers, financial intermediaries play a key role in financial markets. Bonding transactions lowers costs by lowering the likelihood of cheating or stealing. Competitive financial intermediaries—namely banks and stockbrokers, rather than grocery store clerks—tend to discover the most efficient ways of completing transactions fairly and quickly.

Imagine one person wants to borrow at a nominal interest rate of 5 percent and another wants to lend at that same rate. These two should meet, specify terms, and write the contract. If they could do that, they would be better off. But if the parties don't know each other, they don't know where the other person is, and they don't even know if the other person is willing to lend or borrow at an acceptable interest rate. These kinds of transaction costs are problematic for borrowers and lenders—like they are for many trades, in and out of financial markets. In places where the asymmetric information between borrowers and lenders who are unknown to each cannot be reduced sufficiently, lending tends to occur primarily between friends, family, and members of the same religious or other affinity group. Borrowers are otherwise apt to renege on the agreement. So, few loans are made in such settings, and economic activity suffers as a result.

That is, there are profit opportunities—from willing lenders and borrowers and other financial actors—but they face transaction costs related to information asymmetries. Moreover, they are willing to pay to resolve such problems. Banks and other financial intermediaries become the middlemen that provide such goods. Banks provide a relatively secure place for borrowers and lenders to aid each other indirectly: the latter by depositing money in the bank, and the former by going to the bank when they need to fund projects or deals. Everyone involved is better off. Lenders earn interest on their deposits, borrowers receive loans when merited, and the bank earns the spread—the difference between the interest paid by borrowers and the interest paid to depositors. The expertise bankers develop—generally in accepting deposits and making loans—earns them a comparative advantage in providing these goods.

Despite our common notion of banks—with pristine Greek columns and marble surfaces denoting stability and security—banks have taken various forms. When large portions of overall economic activity took place at markets and fairs, people who exchanged currency could set up shop and provide their banking services. That is, money changers developed a comparative advantage in what we often consider to be banking services, for example, evaluating and exchanging currency, accepting and securing deposits, and lending. Greek banks in the fourth and fifth century, for example, took the form of triangular tables where money could be easily exchanged and where calculations were recorded. The modern Greek word for bank is derived from these tables, *trapeza* (Goetzmann 2017, 82).

London goldsmiths in the latter half of the 17th century also developed a comparative advantage in banking. In particular, they issued paper notes redeemable for the gold deposited with them (Kim 2011). Goldsmiths realized they could issue more paper notes than actual gold on hand because the notes were more convenient to use in transactions than gold itself. By lending the paper notes, they could earn seigniorage, or profits from the issuance of money.

Banking even arises in places where people eschew modern conveniences but still want to borrow and lend. In Amish communities, for example, access to financial markets and, in particular, banking can help build a larger home for a growing family, alleviate the consequences of a poor harvest, and cover unexpected expenses. While the upshots of banking seem clear, the Amish might be unable to access *regular* banking services—many do not have a formal credit score, live far urban areas where most banks are found, and cannot use Internet banking (Wright 2019b). But because banking is competitive, some banks wanted their business, unusual as it might be. *Bank of Bird-in-Hand*—now one of the healthiest banks in the country—catered to the Amish by expanding their drive-in windows to accommodate the horse and buggies the Amish rely on for transportation and by creating a mobile bank that travels throughout Amish communities (Smith and Rafieyan 2018).

And They Wear Many Hats

Financial intermediaries provide many goods and enhance financial markets in many ways. Aside from a source of credit and deposits, banks pool resources and diversify risk, provide access to financial services and liquidity, and alleviate information asymmetry problems. By doing so, these intermediaries become a source of financial innovation and lower the costs of accessing financial markets.

They Pool Resources and Diversify Risk

Financial intermediaries accumulate funds from many people as they provide their goods. This pool of funds allows the firm to expand, from which they discover ways to lower costs. For example, instead of writing individual loan contracts for each person—which might be appropriate when a bank services a handful of loans per month—a standardized contract facilitates lending for a larger number of borrowers and speeds up the review process. An investment firm that gathers funds from a pool of investors can purchase a greater number of stocks than a single investor; moreover, the investment firm can purchase those stocks at a lower price per share, or they might be able to purchase with a discount because of the large purchase.

Consider insurance companies, financial intermediaries that pool resources from myriad policyholders via premiums in exchange for making payments under predetermined conditions like a property loss. Providing insurance would be expensive if the insurance company only issued a handful of policies. In such a case, even a few, but unexpectedly large, number of legitimate claims might leave the insurer with more costs than revenue. Expanding the pool of clients, however, brings in more revenue than the additional costs. In other words, there are economies of scale at play, and also the law of large numbers.

As the pool of funds becomes larger and as it is derived from a more diverse population, financial intermediaries bear less risk. If a bank only lent to farmers, for example, or if an insurance company only granted policies to factory workers, all their eggs go into one basket. The firm bears a larger amount of risk particular to the specific group of borrowers. If many farmers default on their loans—because they had a bad harvest and they didn't purchase futures—the bank that originated those loans will lose assets. This kind of risk becomes more manageable as most commercial banks—even the smallest banks—accumulate deposits from tens of thousands to millions of lenders and they make loans to tens of thousands or even millions of borrowers. Bird-in-Hand caters to the Amish, for example, but does not deal with them exclusively as they are too few and too concentrated in a few industries.

They Increase Access and Liquidity

Banks want to provide deposits and credit; insurance companies want to provide coverage as inexpensively as possible. In competitive markets, financial intermediaries face incentives to innovate and to provide greater access to financial markets. Banks also compete on product variety. Banks offer simple savings accounts, but also certificates of deposits and longer-term savings accounts where deposits give up some liquidity for yield. And as computing power continues to advance, the digitization of banking means people have easier and cheaper access to banking services.

The advent of peer-to-peer lending after 2010 via firms like Prosper and LendingClub makes it even easier for people to lend and borrow—and to find more agreeable interest rates. Not only can people borrow more easily, they can shop around for lower rates or for loans with different payout periods. This kind of customization can make people better off in many ways. For example, people can acquire loans worth thousands of dollars from their phones in a relatively short timeframe. People have access to a much more global credit market than when they only had a handful of loan officers in town.

As financial intermediaries develop and attract customers, they achieve lower per unit costs and can pass some of the savings onto their customers eager to exchange currencies, stocks, bonds, and derivatives. Investment funds, for example, use their cost advantages to attract more investors.

They Mitigate Information Asymmetry, So We Can Move On

Information asymmetry arises when people in an exchange have different information about the quality of the goods being exchanged or about the qualities of a prospective partner. Even in a world where we have supercomputers in our pockets, information asymmetries suffuse markets because they are inherent aspects of reality. Severe information asymmetries discourage exchange, and can unravel markets.

Information asymmetries distort how markets typically function because the party with superior information might take advantage of the party with inferior information. Any party who faces this problem—whether they are benevolent or nefarious—will face incentives to behave in ways that distort markets.

Financial intermediaries have developed mechanisms for reducing information asymmetry, especially when intermediaries compete against other intermediaries. Banks and loan officers, for example, develop a comparative advantage in evaluating the likelihood borrowers will pay their debts. The more banks select safer borrowers, the more revenue they earn from lending, all else equal.

A Many-Headed Serpent

The main kinds of information asymmetry include *adverse selection, moral hazard*, and *the principal–agent problem*.

Adverse Selection

This kind of information asymmetry arises when two parties have different information about the value of a potential exchange. A classic example of adverse selection is the market for used cars or *lemons*, where the asymmetry centers on the quality of a used car (Akerlof 1970). Whereas the seller of a car knows a great deal about the car's quality, a buyer does not. A seller might know, for example, how hard their car was used, how sharply corners were turned, and how well their car was maintained. Because the asymmetry is costly if not impossible to mitigate, buyers develop expectations used cars will be lemons, even if some are good *peaches*.

This asymmetry makes negotiations difficult for buyers and sellers. If you are selling an objectively good used car—one that you've maintained and barely driven—you might be unable to convince a willing buyer to make a deal. As a result, exchanges are less likely, and the market might fizzle out. Akerlof (1970) formalizes this by suggesting that buyers decrease the maximum price they are willing to pay based on the average quality of cars. As a result, owners of above-average cars—cars with a price above what a buyer is willing to pay—tend to exit the market. This effect decreases the quality of cars in the remaining pool, which lowers a buyer's maximum price they are willing to pay, which pushes more sellers out, and so on. The market unravels if adverse selection remains a problem.

Adverse selection problems can wreak havoc on financial markets too. Bank managers face this problem when they consider loan applicants. Whereas applicants know much more about whether they are thrifty and how they plan to use funds, it might be impossible for a loan officer to acquire this information from a credible source. As this asymmetry persists, the bank might judge applicants based on the average riskiness of the pool of applicants. As such, interest rates might be higher than otherwise. When thrifty Tom and Tamara walk in to ask for a loan, they might be unwilling to pay such high rates. If they leave the pool, the average risk of default rises, which encourages the bank to raise rates even further.

Moral Hazard

This kind of information asymmetry follows when two parties have different information about the value of an exchange that has already been consummated. Moral hazard problems change the incentives people face, which can encourage them to renege on a deal, to spend more than they would have otherwise, or behave in ways contrary to the original deal. If I were to insure my house against fire, for example, the insurance company might agree to pay all damages. Moral hazard might not lead me to purposefully start a fire, but I might be less careful about where I put candles, checking the smoke alarm, and so on.

Moral hazard problems arise in loan markets, too. Loan officers, for example, want to grant loans they expect will be paid back. While a bank might extend a $50,000 loan to build your business, you might decide to spend the money to throw a lavish party, or to hire more employees than you promised to, or would have if spending your own money. This incentive to spend—because you've received the loan and the loan officer might be unable to observe your spending habits—encourages behaviors that weren't a part of the original loan.

The Principal–Agent Problem

The principal–agent problem is a kind of moral hazard problem that arises when an employee or other agent behaves in his or her own best interest instead of in the best interest of the principal or the owner of a firm. This is especially the case when it is difficult for a principal to monitor an agent's actions. If we view the shareholders of a company as the principal and the CEO of that company as the agent, we can better understand some of the problems that plague corporate governance. That is, the principals want to increase the value of their shares, and they have charged the CEO to make that happen. The problem is that the CEO wants to pursue other goals, for example, to increase her own remuneration, which might come at the expense of the goals of the principals. With many external factors that also influence the value of a firm and the value of shares, it is difficult to directly monitor the behavior of CEOs (Traflet and Wright 2022).

Financial Intermediaries Slay, Again and Again

While transaction costs and information asymmetry problems seem burdensome, financial intermediaries face incentives to minimize the burden. Insurance companies, for example, are rewarded when they can better evaluate the quality of applicants, which minimizes the adverse selection problem. Life insurers attempt to learn a great deal about the health of potential insureds. Life insurers know your age and weight and prior medical conditions. They might even ask for medical records and tests, which further reduce asymmetry. With this information—along with actuarial tables—life insurers can devise a relatively accurate assessment of how and when people with various traits will die, on average. By providing their goods and minimizing information asymmetries, insurers attract more premium dollars while not underpricing the risks they choose to accept.

Car insurance companies also face incentives to resolve moral hazard problems. The problem is that once drivers are insured, they might drive more recklessly, which means paying more claims than expected. With advances in monitoring technology, however, many insurers can offer discounts to drivers who voluntarily reveal information about driving habits. Such monitors report real-time information like driving speeds and whether there were abrupt stops or sharp turns. Such innovations align incentives to reward safer driving, which reduces moral hazard problems.

Commercial banks use various techniques to minimize asymmetry problems. From simple face-to-face communication and standardized forms, loan officers can learn a lot about people and their riskiness. The more people develop a reputation or history with a bank, the better the bank can evaluate loan applications. Banks can examine the spending habits of customers when they are evaluating the risk of default and when they are ensuring the loan is being used appropriately. Banks also use restrictive covenants that specify how people can use loans. Many banks specialize in offering financial services to specialized clients, for example, teacher's credit unions or Amish farmers, allowing them to develop expertise in the problems such borrowers might present.

The use of collateral—property pledged for repayment in the event of default—is another way banks can reduce information asymmetry problems. That is, by asking a potential borrower for an asset that is a portion of the overall value of the loan, lenders are assured some portion of the loan in the event of default. Putting up one's house, for example, is a kind of collateral that aligns incentives, signals borrower quality, and discourages borrowers from using funds inappropriately.

Principal–agent problems seem difficult in the context of corporate governance. Managing a corporation is complicated, and there are myriad reasons why a firm might increase or decrease in value. If the CEO knows this, she might use this to her advantage, for example, to put in less effort or to direct resources to her benefit. Shareholders, though, have some ways to monitor and influence CEO behavior. Relatively large salaries tend to align incentives; that is, the CEO will earn a large wage—or a bonus or stock options—if the CEO's actions result in higher profits and hence larger dividends or higher stock prices. Outside audits paid for by stockholders can help in the most egregious cases of executive fraud (Traflet and Wright 2022).

Competition Is Key

The problems caused by asymmetric information are commonplace, but so are the solutions financial intermediaries discover to lower transaction costs, elicit information, and monitor behavior, especially when they face a related profit motive. Competition provides a clear setting through which firms face this profit motive. When firms lack such motives, they are less likely to produce goods that customers value.

As Robert argues elsewhere, competition played an integral role in the development of American financial markets (Wright 2002b; 2002a). When firms, banks, and other public and private corporations sold stocks to customers directly, for example, competition encouraged firms to communicate with potential investors via newspaper advertisements, word of mouth, and the publication of prospectuses. This competitive setting encouraged the formation of balance sheets that accurately reflected a firm's worth and stock prices that accurately reflected that worth (along with relevant supply and demand conditions). Investing remained local given the transaction costs and information problems, but local and regional financial markets were competitive and a substantial source of credit.

Regulations that limit competition sever the link between the profit motive and serving the interests of customers. For example, New Deal legislation like the Securities Act of 1933 and the Banking Act of 1933—crafted and written by larger securities and investment banks—raised the costs of purchasing stocks, for example, during an initial public offering, for everyone, except for larger banks. These kinds of rules create perverse, long-lasting incentives and serve the interests of the few at the expense of the many. For example, investment banks now face incentives to undervalue their stock during an IPO. If the market value of a stock is $20 per share, but investment bankers offer it at $15, the bankers and corporate insiders can offer this profit opportunity to friends for a small cut.

Financial intermediaries are imperfect, and they are never going to completely resolve the problems associated with asymmetric information. The key to understanding these firms is that they are more likely to discover solutions when they face incentives to do so. Such incentives are primarily found in competitive markets where the costs to enter and exit are negligible and where individuals have expectations of earning net revenue.

CHAPTER 10

Depository Institutions

We now dive deeper into the mechanics of banking—one of the most important kinds of financial intermediation. Once we recognize how costly it is for people to change currencies or transform their wealth, for example, from cash to more remunerative assets, we recognize the usefulness of banks and how they play an integral role in financial systems.

A Centuries-Old Practice

Banks pursue profitability in a unique way, by transforming liabilities into assets and *vice-versa*. Liabilities are sums owed to others like the money due to depositors. Assets are sums owed by others, like the interest and principal to be repaid by borrowers. Liabilities are the source of funds, the means by which banks purchase assets. The difference between the dollar (monetary) value of assets and liabilities equals the bank's equity, alternatively known as its net worth or capital:

$$Assets - Liabilities = Equity$$

But a bank's balance sheet tells only part of its story. Its income statement is also important. Like other businesses, banks have sources of revenue, mostly interest paid on loans or securities, and expenses, its operating expenses (salaries, electricity, etc.), taxes, and regulatory compliance costs. It also has to pay depositors and others that have lent it money. A bank might pay depositors and its other creditors 5 percent per year, while getting 10 percent from its borrowers. The difference is known as the *gross spread*, not because it is nasty, but because it doesn't account for taxes and other costs of doing business.

Bankers can earn a gross spread because depositors want a relatively secure place to store money and an easy and inexpensive way to make payments to others. Borrowers want relatively quick and easy access to credit, often large amounts of it. All types of banks—commercial, community, regional and super-regional, money center, universal, and depository institutions not called banks, like savings and loans, mutual savings banks, and credit unions—foster the expectation that they are the least expensive and most convenient place for depositors and borrowers to find each other.

Successful banking is not easy, and banks often compete vigorously for both depositors and borrowers. The best way to begin to think about the challenges facing bank managers is to examine bank balance sheets. For example, Table 10.1 shows a bank that has $1,000 in deposits, from which it keeps $100 in reserves and lends the remainder.

It is simplified down to its essence. Table 10.2 lists the main categories of assets and liabilities for commercial banks in the United States and the magnitude of these forms on December 8, 2021.

The balance sheets of individual banks change frequently as people deposit into and withdraw from various checking and savings accounts, as people borrow, and as a bank acquires other assets and liabilities. Whereas a balance sheet shows a snapshot of a bank's assets and liabilities at a given

Table 10.1 A balance sheet

Assets	Liabilities
$100 (reserves)	$1,000 (deposits)
$950 (loans)	$50 (capital)

Table 10.2 Assets and liabilities of commercial banks in the United States (as of December 8, 2021)

Assets	Billions of USD	Percent	Liabilities	Billions of USD	Percent
Loans	10,656.3	46.9	Deposits	17,936.2	86.4
Securities	5,628.7	24.8	Capital	1,956.7	9.4
Cash	4,160.9	18.3	Borrowings	1,706.7	8.2
Other assets	1,807.1	8.0	Other liabilities	933.9	4.5

Source: Board of Governors of the Federal Reserve System.

point in time, *t-accounts* show how those columns change as assets and liabilities change in the course of business. Table 10.3 shows a t-account for a bank that received a $1,000 deposit. Table 10.4 shows how to record a $500 withdrawal.

Banking Is a Balancing Act Between Risk...

Bank management is more involved than merely accepting deposits and making loans. Both deposits and lending comprise significant portions of a bank's assets and liabilities, but there are other kinds of assets and liabilities. Moreover, the transformation process between assets and liabilities creates various types of risk that might lead to insolvency (insufficient reserves) or bankruptcy (liabilities > assets). Figures 10.1 and 10.2 show the different categories of commercial bank assets and liabilities, respectively, in the United States.

Banks issue short-term, relatively liquid, safe liabilities and transform them into long-term, relatively illiquid, risky assets. For example, banks accept deposits in the form of cash—not computers or houses—with the expectation that a checking account depositor can withdraw it all at will without penalty or delay. Depositors find this kind of liquidity, security, and ease so beneficial that banks often pay little if any interest on checking and other transaction accounts. Depositor dollars can be aggregated and used to finance businesses and governments. If banking sounds like an easy way to get rich, however, keep in mind that much can go wrong.

Table 10.3 A t-account (deposit)

Assets	Liabilities
+$100 (reserves)	+$1,000 (deposits)
+$900 (loans)	

Table 10.4 A t-account (withdrawal)

Assets	Liabilities
-$500 (reserves)	-$500 (deposits)

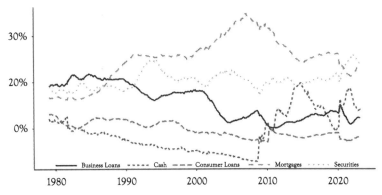

Figure 10.1 U.S. commercial bank assets, 1973 to 2023

Source: FRED database using fredr.

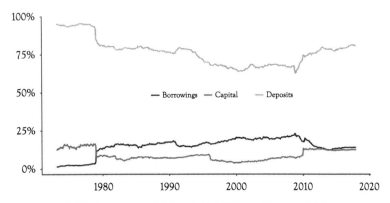

Figure 10.2 U.S. commercial bank liabilities, 1973 to 2017

Source: FRED database using fredr.

Liquidity, Credit, and Trading Risk

Banks face multiple kinds of risk. Liquidity risk arises when banks *borrow short and lend long*, as they use deposits that they have to repay immediately to fund loans that run for weeks, months, or even years. Bankers also must manage credit risk, the probability that a borrower defaults and repays only a portion of the sum borrowed. Lending to a new startup, for example, increases the assets of a bank and provides funds for the startup, but many new companies default. A failure to repay would reduce the bank's assets and thus reduce its capital/net worth. Banks face trading risk when the price of a newly acquired asset differs from when it is sold. Today, under mark-to-market accounting, a bank that purchased $1,000,000 worth of bonds loses assets and net worth as the market value of those bonds falls. (In the past, some financial intermediaries could account for the bonds at their purchase or historical price, or face value, so long as the drop in market price was due solely to market interest rate increases and not a default or downgrade.)

Interest Rate Risk

When banks acquire assets and liabilities that are sensitive to changing interest rates, the value of those assets and liabilities change as interest rates change. This is called interest rate risk. For example, if depositors demand higher interest rates on their checking or savings accounts, the cost of acquiring liabilities rises. To develop this problem with more detail, consider the balance sheet in Table 10.5.

This bank has interest rate-sensitive liabilities and assets, namely variable rate certificate of deposits (CDs) and variable rate short-term loans, respectively. This risk arises when interest rates change. If interest rates rise enough, the cost of servicing liabilities will become more than what the bank earns from its assets. If interest rates fall, the cost of servicing liabilities will become less than what the bank earns from its assets.

A simple way to analyze how changing interest rates influence profitability is through *gap analysis*, or by considering the difference between rate-sensitive assets (A_r), rate-sensitive liabilities (L_r), and the change in interest rates. Thus, a bank's change in profit ($\Delta\pi$)—due to a change in interest rates—equals

$$\Delta\pi = (A_r - L_r) * \Delta i$$

Table 10.5 An interest rate-sensitive balance sheet

Assets	Liabilities
$1,000 (variable rate, short-term loan)	$2,000 (variable rate CDs)
$5,000 (fixed rate, long-term loan)	$3,000 (checkable deposits)

Using the balance sheet in Table 10.5, for example, if the change in interest rates equals a positive 10 percent, $\Delta\pi = -\$1,000 * 0.1 = -\$100$. If instead the bank had \$2,000 in variable rate, short-term loans, all else equal, it would not experience any change in profit as interest rates increased because there would be no gap, or difference, in its variable rate assets and liabilities.

The risks of banking are worrisome, but bankers have strong incentives, the profit motive, to manage their accounts to minimize such risks. The classic movie *It's a Wonderful Life* (1946) highlights some of these issues and solutions. In particular, the scene where George Bailey calms his panic-stricken customers highlights the challenge every banker faces regarding liquidity risk. Bailey informs his customers how a bank works, that is, their money is not physically at the bank, but it is being used to build the homes of their neighbors. If banks do not consistently transform liabilities into assets and *vice-versa* such that they can meet the demands of depositors, clients might want to take their funds elsewhere. The bank run Bailey faces in the movie can make a bank insolvent and can lead to cascade effects whereby people believe other banks are insolvent regardless of whether they actually are. Mary Hatch, Bailey's wife, saves the day, if only temporarily. Mary keeps the bank open by taking the \$2,000 she and George would have spent on their honeymoon and provides a private, emergency liquidity loan to Bailey Building & Loan. George's calming presence and Mary's loan assures customers that the bank is solvent.

In their efforts to remain profitable and to continuously transform assets and liabilities, banks want to maintain a diverse set of assets and liabilities, a sufficient amount of liquidity, and a sufficient amount of capital. Each of these goals entails a tradeoff.

Managing Liquidity

Maintaining liquidity refers to banks keeping enough reserves on hand to meet the demand from depositors, but not too much that they aren't able to create assets. For example, the bank in Table 10.4 might be able to cover a withdrawal of \$500, but in so doing, its reserves decrease. Such a withdrawal might mean the bank is unable to cover the next withdrawal, or that it is left with an amount of reserves below what a regulator deems appropriate.

To resolve potential liquidity problems, bankers want to increase their reserve–deposit ratio in the least costly manner available. They could sell assets, for example, loans, securities, branches, and put those funds into reserves, but doing so is costly. Selling loans to another bank, for example, is possible, but the value of the loan to another bank might be less than what the originating bank anticipated because of information asymmetry problems or an increase in interest rates since loan origination. Selling assets like equities and branches depends on market prices. Some of these assets, like branches, might take months to sell and require paying a hefty commission. A superior option might be to encourage depositors to keep their deposits with the bank, which might require raising the interest rate on deposits, lowering fees for services, and by improving the quality of their goods. A bank might also borrow to increase its reserve–deposit ratio—derived from investors, banks, or from central banks—which entails paying interest.

Managing Diversity in Assets and Liabilities

Bankers want to maintain a diverse portfolio of assets and liabilities, from which they can have their desired amount of liquidity, risk, and return. For example, using 100 percent of a bank's deposits to make 30-year loans will end in disaster if gross deposits decrease, which is not unusual. Making loans with a variety of maturities, by contrast, will allow the bank to better meet net deposit outflows. There are many ways to render bank balance sheets more diverse. Banks might purchase government bonds because they will be easily sold in the event of unexpected withdrawals. Banks can also diversify their pool of loans by lending in new geographical or business areas. Similarly, banks issue a diverse set of liabilities, from short-term deposits to long-term negotiable CDs.

One of the more effective means of reducing credit risks is to screen applications to reduce adverse selection. That is, bankers learn more about potential borrowers through conversation and application forms, which can become binding parts of a loan contract. Borrowers that misrepresent their ability to repay a loan can find their loan rescinded and even face legal penalties. Banks can also attenuate credit risk via specialization or lending to particular kinds of borrowers. Forming long-term relationships with borrowers also helps to resolve information asymmetry problems and limits credit risk. Banks develop such relationships by offering better rates to previous, successful borrowers or to customers that have checking or savings accounts with the bank. Collateral and lines of credit also encourage borrowers to pay their debts on time.

Managing Rate Sensitivity

Another aspect of acquiring a diverse set of assets and liabilities is to examine how sensitive a balance sheet is to changing interest rates. The more sensitive a balance sheet is to rate changes, the more a bank might be interested in actively managing their gap. If interest rates are expected to rise, for example, banks could decrease the duration of assets so that the interest rate can be renegotiated frequently; they can also decrease the cost of their liabilities by increasing the duration so that their creditors are locked in to relatively low, old interest rates for longer periods. Similarly, as discussed, banks can alter the duration of rate-sensitive assets and liabilities.[1]

Managing Capital

Finally, a bank can manage its capital, the cushion of equity that helps it to avoid bankruptcy caused by the burdens of various regulatory changes or shocks to financial markets. More capital, all else equal, makes a bank safer but there is an opportunity cost to holding capital, which necessitates a tradeoff between profit, as measured by return on equity (ROE), and stability.

Measuring Risk and Reward

The profitability of bank can be measured and compared in two major ways. First, the ROA shows the ratio between a bank's net after-tax revenue and its total assets.

---

[1] More sophisticated approaches consider differences in the duration of assets and liabilities. For example, duration analysis accounts for the duration of a bond and multiplies that by the percentage-point change in the interest rate.

$$ROA = \frac{Net\ after\ tax\ Revenue}{Total\ Assets}$$

This measure represents how a bank uses its assets to create profit. The larger the ratio, the better a bank is at using its assets to create revenue, a measure of particular interest to economists. Second, we can measure a bank's return on equity (ROE), which shows the ratio between a bank's net after-tax revenue and its capital.

$$ROE = \frac{Net\ after\ tax\ Revenue}{Capital}$$

This measure shows how effectively a bank uses its capital—which is important to the owners of the bank's stock. The larger the ratio, the more effectively a bank is at using its capital. While a bank's ROA and its ROE measures its profitability, these measures also shed light on how leveraged a bank is. Leverage refers to the amount of assets purchased from borrowed funds. The leverage ratio is the amount of a bank's total assets relative to its capital. The higher the leverage ratio, the more likely the bank is to fail, all else equal.

$$Leverage\ Ratio = \frac{Bank\ Assets}{Bank\ Capital}$$

Competition Spurs Innovation

When banks compete against other banks for deposits, they become interested in producing goods customers value. Financial rules and regulations, macroeconomic volatility, technology, and bank ownership structure all influence these incentives and the kind of innovation—which we will explore in subsequent chapters—but we should note how useful competition is.

Toasters, Clocks, and Parkas

Accumulating deposits is not as easy as it might seem, especially when there are more attractive alternatives or when regulations prevent offering higher interest rates. In such cases, banks are less able to transform assets and liabilities. To address this problem—where interest rates are not enough to encourage deposits—banks try to attract customers and their deposits in other ways. Nonprice means of competition vary, but they might take the form of offering kitchen appliances, watches, sign-up and referral bonuses, and so on. In the 1970s and 1980s, for example, Twin City Federal based in Minnesota encouraged deposits by offering Timex watches, down-feather parkas, duffle bags, and *Sylvia Porter's Money Book* (its commercials are available on YouTube).

Coffee Shops and Mobile Banking

Today, bankers still face incentives to compete for customers' dollars, partnering with various firms, organizations, and schools to encourage deposits and lower costs. Capital One recently partnered with Peets Coffee to construct a joint bank branch and coffee shop. Each store shares the fixed costs of operating a store and subsidizes each other's operations. Moreover, Capital One shoppers receive special discounts and offers at the cafe.

Throughout the world, technology has dramatically changed how people access the commercial banking industry. The advent of cellphones and mobile banking has encouraged people to easily and securely deposit funds, transfer those funds, and accumulate savings. For instance, Figure 10.3 shows the growth of mobile money in Kenya, a country of

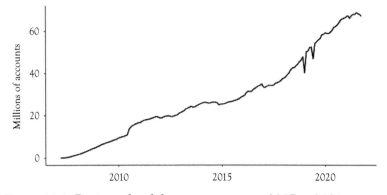

Figure 10.3 Registered mobile money accounts, 2007 to 2021

Source: Central Bank of Kenya.

56 million people. Between 2010 and 2020, the number of registered mobile banking accounts grew by a factor of 6. Such technological developments along with banks' ability to transform assets and liabilities spur economic development and improve standards of living (Burns 2018).

And Even Money

Competition in banking also produces money—as in a stable, reliable means of exchange. When banks are allowed to issue their own currencies or receipts for deposits, they compete with other banks. This competitive process gives bankers an incentive to maintain the value of their currency (see, for example, Selgin 1988; White 1996). If bankers issue too much of their currency—so that its purchasing power falls—depositors will begin to withdraw from the bank. If bankers issue too few of their currency—so they acquire too few assets and decrease what they pay to depositors—depositors will also begin to withdraw from the bank. As we learned, this withdrawal process can shrink the balance sheet of a bank. Thus, bankers face incentives to issue an amount of money according to the demands of customers.

Competition Also Means Fewer Banks and Better Banking

One of the more striking features of the U.S. banking industry is the decline in the number of commercial banks and the concentration of total assets in larger banks. Rather than indications of growing monopoly power, such trends indicate growing competition. This is especially because unit banks—banks without branches—faced relatively little competition for most of the 20th century. Figure 10.4 shows the consistent decline in the number of commercial banks in the United States.

Such trends reflect bank failures as well as mergers and acquisitions. For example, the Federal Deposit Insurance Corporation reports 364 failed banks since 2000. Figure 10.5 shows two recent waves of failures, one associated with the Savings-and-Loans crisis and one associated with the Global Financial Crisis of 2008. But most of the decline in the number of banks is due to mergers encouraged by regulatory reforms in the 1990s (Wright and Sylla 2015).

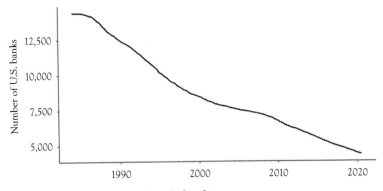

Figure 10.4 The decline of U.S. banking

Source: FRED database using fredr.

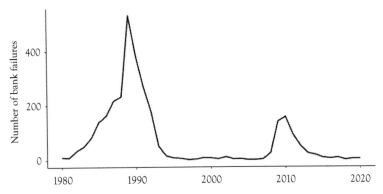

Figure 10.5 Annual bank failures in the United States, 1980 to 2020

Source: FRED database using fredr.

Technological developments, deregulation, and an increasingly global banking sector all explain how the banking sector has become more competitive. Advances in data collection and communications technology—beginning in the 1970s and continuing today with the Internet and smartphones—mean banks can more cheaply mitigate some types of information asymmetry problems. Moreover, people can access their checking accounts, loans, and myriad other financial services with finger clicks on phone screens.

The repeal of banking regulations also plays an important part in the decline in the number of banks. That is, repealing some of these regulations leads to a more connected banking sector, far from the world of unit banking. Such a transition encourages competition and the decline of less profitable banks. Between 1927 and 1994, for example, owning a bank branch outside of the state a bank received its charter, or was headquartered if a national bank, was illegal due to the McFadden Act of 1927. Such rules—enforced by courts—forbade the operation of automated teller machines (ATMs) and armored trucks as mobile banks (First Nat'l Bank in Plant City v. Dickinson, 396 U.S. 122, 1969; "Independent Bankers Ass'n v. Marine Midland Bank," 583 F. Supp. 1042, W.D.N.Y., 1984). Similarly, the Gramm-Leach-Bliley Act of 1999 eliminated a restriction dating from the 1930s that forbid mergers between commercial banks, insurance, and investment firms.

People are not beholden to local banks or even the banks within their country. Similarly, banks are not beholden to liabilities and assets from a concentrated geographical area. Perhaps global banking is more useful for clients engaged in international trade, but such competition encourages banks to improve the quality of their goods or exit the market.

PART IV

The Economics of Central Banking and Monetary Policy

CHAPTER 11

The Money Supply Process and Money Multipliers

One of the most important facets of the banking system is how it creates money. The money creation process develops across multiple actors and choices within the banking system, which primarily includes banks—who act as lenders and as depository institutions—and economic entities (individual people, businesses, and governments)—who act as borrowers and as depositors. Central banks are another important actor in this process—as they attempt to use the tools of monetary policy to alter the money supply. While central banks often try to influence the money supply, for example, in response to crises like the Great Depression, the Great Recession, and COVID-19, we will now describe the economics of the money creation process, which means focusing on the choices economic entities make regarding the amount and type of money they wish to hold.

Banks Create Money

Our ultimate objective is to understand how individuals and banks influence the money supply. We need to define terms before we can adequately answer this question. The most important component of the money supply is the monetary base, MB. It equals the amount of currency (paper notes and coins) in circulation, C, and the total amount of reserves in the banking system, R. These components of MB depend on the choices economic entities make, for example, to borrow, to spend, to deposit, and so on, and the choices banks make, for example, to lend and accept deposits and hold reserves. Figure 11.1 shows how the amount of currency in circulation and bank reserves influence the monetary base and, ultimately, the money supply MS as measured by $M1$.

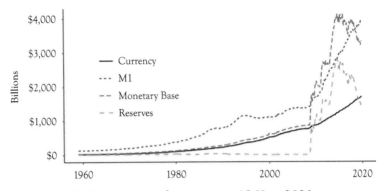

Figure 11.1 *U.S. money supply estimates, 1960 to 2020*

Source: FRED database using fredr.

Increases (decreases) in *MB* lead to increases (decreases) in the *MS*. Moreover, the *MS* is larger than the *MB*, and changes in the *MS* do not always follow from changes in the *MB*.

One generally recognized set of factors that influences the *MS* is known as the money creation process. This process begins when banks lend, which sets off a chain reaction that multiplies the *MS*. As the borrower spends the proceeds of a loan, those funds circulate throughout the economy through everyday economic activities, that is, buying and selling goods. Some economic entities will deposit funds they receive into a bank, increasing the bank's liabilities and allowing it to acquire additional assets subject to its desired amount of reserves. In other words, the original bank loan allows other banks to make additional loans. As a result, additional money is created.

This entire process can be represented by the t-account for a single bank, shown in Table 11.1. Recall that each line records a change in assets and/or liabilities. For simplicity, we assume there is only one bank in an

Table 11.1 *The money creation process*

Assets	Liabilities
+ Loan A	
+ Loan B	+ Deposit A
+ Loan C	+ Deposit B
...	...

economy, which means it made the initial loan and it is the only bank to receive deposits. Also, note that after each deposit, a bank must lend less than the full amount received on deposit in order to maintain its desired amount of reserves. Thus, $A > B > C$.

Imagine a bank sells some of its securities for $1,000,000, and it already has what it deems to be sufficient reserves. The money received for the securities is excess, that is, more than its desired amount. A borrower takes the loan and starts to spend; she starts renting factory space, a store front, equipment for her business, and hires staff. Notice the variety of people who receive the funds that originally came from the loan: the borrower, the owner of the factory, the owner of the store front, the owner of the equipment, and individual employees. All these entities have experienced an increase in their cash balances, from which they will make additional purchases. Moreover, the increase in cash balances will encourage some to make additional deposits.

At some point, the initial $1,000,000 finds its way back to the bank in the form of deposits. The bank now has additional liabilities, which—as you might recall—they consider *sources of funds*. If the bank wants to hold 10 percent of all deposits in reserves, it can lend $900,000 of the $1 million, and the process begins anew. This time, another person receives a $900,000 loan, spends it, the money circulates, and eventually the $900,000 will be deposited too. The bank can then lend out $810,000, or 10 percent of $900,000. The process continues until the sum becomes too small to lend for a profit. Table 11.2 shows an extended t-account from the initial $1,000,000 loan.

Table 11.2 The money creation process

Assets	Liabilities
+ $1,000,000	
+ $900,000	+ $1,000,000
+ $810,000	+ $900,000
+ $729,000	+ $810,000
+ $656,100	+ $729,000
+ $590,490	+ $656,100
...	...

Money for Me, Money for You, More Money for Everyone

The money creation process has important implications for economic activity. Primarily, it means economic entities and banks have access to additional funds to lend, borrow, and consummate trades. This process also illuminates the relationship between the monetary base and the supply of money. For any $1 added to the monetary base, the money creation process can create more than $1. Thus,

$$MS = m * MB$$

Where MS is the supply of money, and m is the money multiplier, which represents the money creation process.

Note that the original $1,000,000 loan created approximately $10,000,000 that other people and banks were able to use. You can determine this $10,000,000 by adding all of the changes in the t-account earlier. A simpler way to observe this—and the larger relationship between the monetary base and the money supply—is to recognize that every dollar added to deposits equals the change in reserves divided by the desired amount of reserves.

$$\Delta D = \frac{\Delta R}{r}$$

Where ΔD is the change in deposits, ΔR is the change in reserves, and r is the reserve ratio. We assumed that the reserve ratio was 10 percent, and the initial change in reserves was $1,000,000. Thus, $\Delta D = \frac{1,000,000}{0.1} = \$10,000,000$. In this case, note that $\frac{1}{r} = 10$, and that $\frac{1}{r}$ is a general way to represent the money multiplier.

This description of the money creation process—along with the simple deposit multiplier—is simplified, but it highlights the general characteristics of how an initial loan can expand the amount of money circulating throughout an economy. Moreover, it shows how changes in reserves influence the money supply (deposits and currency in circulation).

With Frictions All Around

Developing a more realistic understanding of the money creation process requires an explicit recognition of the frictions that occur in the real-world.

If banks lend the entirety of excess reserves and if borrowers accept the full amount and if borrowers spend those funds and if the funds are soon deposited and if the process continues, then the simple deposit multiplier is an accurate predictor of money supply expansion. If those conditions are not met, however, the simple multiplier represents an upper-bound estimate of the amount of deposits created due to a change in reserves.

We can develop a more accurate multiplier—and a better idea of how changes in the monetary base change the money supply—by focusing on the frictions identified earlier. These factors curtail the money creation process. A bank might not lend its entire amount of excess reserves. For example, if a central bank pays interest on excess reserves—like the Federal Reserve did in response to the financial crisis of 2007 to 2009—banks will lend fewer reserves, and fewer dollars will circulate. Generally, borrowers might take out loans and spend those funds, but it might take some time—months and years—for those dollars to be deposited back into a bank. As interest rates rise, for example, people are likely to hold lower cash balances. Changes in the amount of reserves a bank is legally required to hold—as determined by a government or central bank—also are relevant, to the extent they are binding, as they curtail the money creation process.

All these factors indicate that the simple deposit multiplier should be amended. Let the amount of excess reserves banks hold relative to total deposits equal the excess reserve ratio, $e = \dfrac{ER}{D}$, where ER is the total amount of excess reserves and D is the total amount of deposits. Let the amount of currency in circulation relative to the amount of deposits be the currency-deposit ratio, $c = \dfrac{C}{D}$, where C is the total amount of currency in circulation.

Using these ratios that indicate frictions in the money creation process, the following formula describes a relatively more sophisticated money multiplier:

$$m = \frac{1+c}{c+e+r}$$

Notice that this multiplier is the same as the previous multiplier if c and e equal zero.

Figure 11.2 shows how c, r, and e change over time, whereas Figure 11.3 shows the corresponding changes in m for M1.

While Figure 11.3 shows how the M1 multiplier changes, we often want to know how broader measures of money change in response to

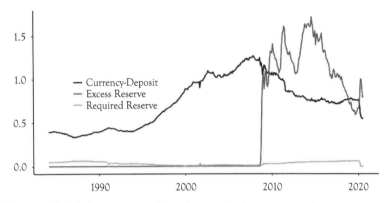

Figure 11.2 The currency-deposit, required reserve, and excess reserve ratio, 1984 to 2020

Source: FRED database using fredr.

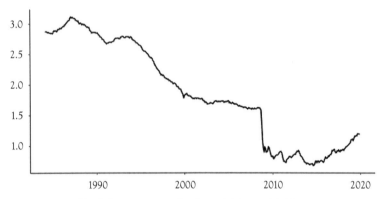

Figure 11.3 The M1 money multiplier, 1984 to 2019

Source: FRED database using fredr.

individuals and banks. For example, M2 represents M1—currency and checkable deposits—plus long-term savings deposits, T, and money market funds and deposits accounts and overnight loans, MMF. This broader money varies less with temporary changes in prices, interest rates, inflation, and output. The multiplier for M2, m_2, includes the frictions previously mentioned and those related to T and MMF. In particular, if people extend the amount of time they make deposits, which increases T, banks have additional long-term liabilities they are responsible for and additional assets they can lend. Thus, as the amount of T relative to D—known as the time-deposit ratio t_d—we expect m_2 to rise. Similarly, if people channel their deposits into money market funds and related deposit accounts, banks have additional funds to lend and expand the money creation process. Thus, as the amount of *MMF* relative to *D*— known as the money market ratio *mmf*—we expect m_2 to rise. Accounting for these factors leads to the following formula for the M2 multiplier:

$$m_2 = \frac{1 + c + t_d + mmf}{c + e + r}$$

Figure 11.4 shows how m_2 changes over time.

We can now derive some of the key factors that influence changes in the money supply. These include changes in the monetary base *MB* and changes in the money multiplier, which include changes in c, r, e, t_d, and *mmf*. Table 11.3 lists these factors, the primary actor that changes it, and the effect those changes have on the money supply.

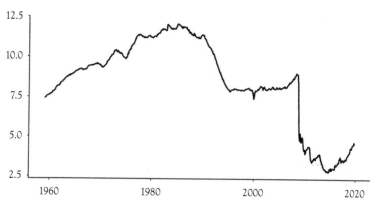

Figure 11.4 The M2 money multiplier, 1959 to 2019

Source: FRED database using fredr.

Table 11.3 Individuals, commercial banks, and the Central Bank influence the money supply

Primary actor	Factors	Effect on money supply	Type
Individuals	↑c	↑/↓	M1 and M2
Individuals	↑t_d	↑	M2
Individuals	↑*mmf*	↑	M2
Commercial banks	↑e	↓	M1 and M2
Central banks	↑r	↓	M1 and M2
Central banks	↑*MB*	↑	M1 and M2

CHAPTER 12

The Economics of Financial Regulation

As marvelous as financial markets are for increasing wealth by connecting borrowers and lenders, spreading risk, and reducing asymmetric information, they can cause problems of their own. Bubbles, shocks, panics, recessions, and other kinds of financial crises can be disastrous because they increase unemployment, disrupt plans, erode life savings, and drive companies into bankruptcy.

The Chicago Board of Exchange (CBOE) publishes an index based on the prices of options, called the VIX, that measures the expectations investors have about the prices of stocks in the S&P 500 over the upcoming 30 days. This forward-looking index measures uncertainty and is generally correlated with periods of recession or sustained periods of falling output and employment. Figure 12.1 shows this relationship with the shaded areas indicating periods of recession.

Moving from left to right, Figure 12.1 illustrates the recessions associated with the Savings and Loans crisis, the dot-com bubble, the Global Financial Crisis, and the COVID-19 epidemic. Domestic inflation and abrupt changes in exchange rates also trigger recessions by disrupting incentives, business plans, and trade. The more such shocks alter the balance sheets of financial intermediaries, the less those intermediaries will be able to perform one of their primary functions, that is, resolving information asymmetry problems.

Bubbles Here and There, Back to the Dutch

Asset bubbles occur when the value of an asset, like a stock, rises above its fundamental value and then falls back to its fundamental value, or lower, over a relatively short period of time. The larger the rise and fall of this bubble, the more people have opportunities to earn and lose wealth. Asset

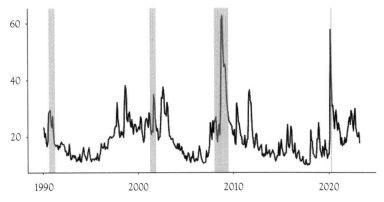

Figure 12.1 The CBOE volatility index, 1990 to 2023

Source: FRED database using fredr.

bubbles happen frequently (Malkiel 2019). But they usually follow periods where demand for an asset rises due to a narrative or story that suggests that the divergence from fundamental value is justified, interest rates fall, credit is easily obtained by using the asset as collateral, there are rapid changes in financial and physical technology that bring inexperienced investors into the market for the frothy asset, or when intermediaries that benefit from trading the asset begin to push it on new investors. Bubbles can grow especially large when there is no easy way to short the frothy asset, or in other words, to profit from a fall in its price, because buyers outnumber sellers, or rather buying pressure outweighs pressure to sell.

If the underlying value (present value of expected future earnings) of Oogle stock is $1,000 per share, but it suddenly doubles or triples, the investors who owned Oogle stock prior to the rise in price become wealthier. If the price continues to rise, people might expect a higher future price and buy the shares solely for that reason. Demand for Oogle stock thus rises faster than the number of shares actively trading in the secondary market. When investors realize that Oogle stock is overpriced—for whatever reason—they begin to short the stock, either formally or by selling their shares. As its price falls, the balance sheets of investors still owning the stock begin to shrink. In other words, their net worth declines, which exacerbates moral hazard, or in other words, the incentive to take on bigger risks, both of which present major problems for lenders.

Lenders are at risk during bubbles as well if they lent on the collateral of the bubbly asset. Investors want to borrow so that they can take full advantage of perceived profit opportunities. If people expect a higher price of Oogle stock in the future, they can borrow today, purchase the stock at a relatively low price, sell when the price is higher, pay back the loan, and keep the remainder. If the price of Oogle stock does not continue to rise, like during the bursting of the asset bubble, investors can be left holding stocks that are worth less than what they were earlier. If they cannot repay the borrowed funds, the lender suffers. Remember the adage, if you cannot repay the bank $10,000, you have a problem; if you cannot repay the bank $1 million, the bank has a problem.

The tulip bulb bubble in the Netherlands during the fall and winter of 1636 to 1637 is well known, but new research on the timing of the bubble provides insight into how bubbles arise (McClure and Thomas 2017). One of the precipitating factors of this bubble—on the actual bulbs and futures contracts of bulb prices—was new technology. By 1635, most bulbs were sold by weight instead of by bulb, which indicated prices more closely aligned with the growth of the bulb and its expected value. Moreover, bulb promissory notes became prominent in 1635. This kind of financial technology facilitated the exchange of bulbs throughout the year and the exchange of notes. Together, these innovations suggest that what we often view as a tulip mania—the crazed rush to purchase tulips—should be viewed as a rational response to new forms of exchange and technology. McClure and Thomas (2017) develop the idea of sequestered capital or capital whose future value cannot be known for some time after an investment must be made, which can lead to a boom and bust cycle. Referencing tulip bulbs, they state that, "Once planted, neither bulb development nor the growth of offsets could be seen … an unknown amount of investment was made in the fall of 1636 into sequestered capital that was literally buried underground." While rampant speculation surrounding bulb prices emerged after planting, it ceased in February 1637 as soon as the bulbs began to sprout. With such information, people could observe which bulbs were going to bloom. Moreover, investors could learn whether bulbs and futures they had purchased earlier in the fall were going to yield positive or negative sums and whether they should sell.

Shocks and Financial Crises

Whereas bubbles impact a particular industry and the damages to balance sheets are relatively contained to that industry, deeper problems arise when financial intermediaries become exposed to bubbles and related shocks. Given the importance of banks and other intermediaries to the financial system, the more they see drastic changes to their balance sheets, the less they can resolve information asymmetry problems, and the more likely recessions will result.

When financial intermediaries face substantial, concurrent requests to pay their creditors (depositors, noteholders, and bondholders)—due to bubbles, sudden rises in interest rates, stock market declines, and governmental fiscal imbalances—they might have to quickly sell a substantial portion of their assets. If many financial intermediaries must sell assets, a downward spiral of prices can have disastrous consequences for individual intermediaries and for the larger financial system. Such shocks leave financial intermediaries with less ability to resolve information asymmetry problems and hence less ability to lend to quality borrowers.

During bank runs, for example, many depositors withdraw their funds all at once; if banks hope to remain in business, they must borrow from others or quickly sell assets. This sell-off lowers asset prices because suddenly sellers outnumber buyers. Even if banks can fend off depositors, the value of their assets shrink as asset prices fall. Banks become much less able, or willing, to lend, which decreases economic activity.

The Global Financial Crisis

In the late 1990s, housing prices began to rise, and at an increasingly fast rate by the mid-2000s. Figure 12.2 shows the Case–Schiller Home Price index, which indicates when the housing bubble developed, and when it burst in 2007, leading to the Great Recession of 2008 to 2009.

The factors described caused the housing bubble: low interest rates, easy credit, commissioned agents incentivized to push large mortgages, numerous entrants into the house *flipping* business, and no easy way to short the market.

The more lenders had mortgages or mortgage-backed securities in the asset columns of their balance sheets, the more their balance sheets swelled during the boom, and the more their balance sheets crumpled during the bust. Many financial intermediaries, including investment banks and pension funds, used mortgage-backed securities and related derivatives as a seemingly safe way to diversify their asset portfolios. The value of

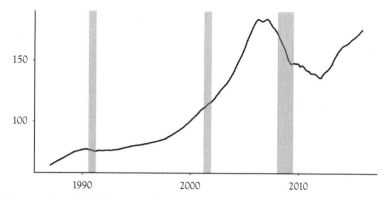

Figure 12.2 *S&P/Case–Shiller U.S. national home price index, 1987 to 2015*

Source: FRED database using fredr.

mortgage-backed securities depended on the value of many mortgages, not just a single one, which diversified risk. In the second half of the decade, however, many people began to default on their mortgages—partly due to lenders making loans to unqualified borrowers because of regulations that encouraged imprudent lending (Wright 2019a). Figure 12.3 shows how the delinquency rate—the dollar amount of delinquent mortgages divided by the dollar amount of total mortgages—began to rise after 2006. In January 2010, the peak delinquency rate, about 11 percent of every dollar in a single-family mortgage was delinquent.

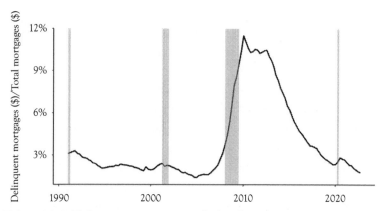

Figure 12.3 *Delinquency rate on single-family mortgages, 1991 to 2022*

Source: FRED database using fredr.

As default rates increased, the value of mortgage-backed securities fell. This lowered the net worth of the financial intermediaries that owned them, which eventually rendered some of them bankrupt.

The Demand for Regulation Takes Many Forms

When banks are prone to runs, when bubbles are likely to form, and when there are credit crunches following panics, people argue they might have been better off—or they might be better prepared for the next shock—if government were to regulate financial intermediaries. Given the variety of bubbles and panics—and the various ways people can be separated from their funds—there are many ways to impose such regulations. Governments can attempt to preempt a bubble by increasing interest rates or tightening credit standards. Regulators can also make some kinds of transactions illegal, or they can penalize or encourage others. Regulators, for example, can penalize fraudulent behavior, forbid some types of intermediaries from purchasing certain types of assets, and subsidize intermediaries deemed too big to fail.

The Dodd–Frank Act and new bureaucracies like the Consumer Financial Protection Bureau were responses to the Global Financial Crisis, but it remains unclear if they can prevent bubbles and crashes. Earlier regulations created in reaction to earlier crises clearly failed to do so. Skeptics argue that many such rules might even make financial markets more prone to instability and failure.

Bankers and Regulators Face Incentives

Public choice theory (see, for example, Mueller 2003; Johnson 1991) suggests that people are people whether they play roles as depositors, bank managers, regulators, bureaucrats in a financial consumer protection agency, or elected officials. Following the economic way of thinking, this seemingly innocuous perspective yields an important insight into how regulators behave: like all people, they respond to incentives.

Public choice economics highlights the incentives people face throughout a political system: voters are rationally ignorant, bureaucrats tend to minimize effort and increase the size and scope of their authority, politicians tend to favor policies that increase the probability of reelection, which often means pursuing goals favored by special interests. Given such incentives, politicians might be more likely to appear to serve the public rather than actually doing so. Regulators might advance policies that enhance their budget and power rather than protecting vulnerable people. Similarly, financial intermediaries might advance their own interests by advocating for rules that restrict competition. Ultimately, public choice economics suggests that it is not at all clear that governmental rules are the panacea advocates claim. While rules might protect some consumers, they might also make only bankers, politicians, or regulators better off.

Nobel prize-winning economist George Stigler developed early public choice approaches to regulation and showed that contrary to the public interest view of government, individuals and firms clamor for government intervention, for example, subsidies and regulations on their own industry, that aid their private interests (Stigler 1971; Peltzman 1993). It makes sense that firms might seek subsidizes, free cash from taxpayers. Supporting regulation of one's own industry, however, seems counterintuitive. By erecting such regulations, however, incumbent firms can make themselves better off by restricting competition from new entrants.

Public choice does not suggest people exclusively pursue their own interests; however, people tend to pursue their own interests when rules and regulations encourage them to do so. Such problems are compounded when voters have many things to do and acquiring information is costly; when special interests reap all the rewards and bear few of the costs of a regulation; and when politicians are self-interested and shortsighted. This logic suggests caution when advocating for additional rules; history shows that regulations typically do more harm than good.

Some Banks Like Regulation

In Chapter 10, we suggested that the presence of regulations, for example, branching regulations, increased the prevalence of unit banking throughout the United States. We can now use the logic of public choice to explain why such rules were imposed in the first place. Restrictions on bank branches and Blue Sky laws—rules that make it illegal or costly to sell securities (an alternative way of obtaining a loan)—are examples of regulations that tend to make incumbent banks better off. The costlier it becomes to enter the banking industry, the fewer competitors there will be, and the more people must use existing banks. The removal of such rules in the 1990s lowered the cost of entering the banking industry, which meant additional competition. Banks now felt the sting of competition as people found alternative ways to access banking services. Similar regulations remain today in the form of restrictions on the kind of assets banks can hold and minimum capital requirements. Such rules might reduce the riskiness of the financial sector on some margins, but also make incumbent banks better off.

Deposit Insurance Faces a Tradeoff Like Every Other Kind of Insurance

Deposit insurance reassures depositors that they will be compensated if an insured bank becomes unable to meet sudden and concurrent demands for deposits, like during a bank run. Congress created the Federal Deposit Insurance Corporation, FDIC, to allay the costs to depositors of bank runs. That sounds like a great regulation but because depositors and bankers do not bear the full costs of a bank run—the FDIC covers losses up to some threshold—they do not have to be as careful. Depositors care less where they deposit their funds, and bankers care less about acquiring cautious investments. In other words, deposit insurance increases banker risk-taking and thus the probability that banks will fail.

Last Resort, Again and Again

The notion of a lender of last resort is intuitive. Providing liquidity to banks and other financial intermediaries in tough times seems reasonable, especially when some financial intermediaries are deemed too-big-to-fail. Such options come with costs, namely higher interest rates and a public signal of losses. Alexander Hamilton developed the basics of last-resort lending during the panic of 1792, that is, the bursting of an asset bubble in U.S. government bonds. His contribution was only recently recognized, however, so *Economist* Editor Walter Bagehot is generally credited for the innovation because he clearly described it in 1873 while referencing the Bank of England. He stated that a lender of last resort should make loans during panics at a penalty rate to any entity that could post sufficient collateral. That rule prevented the many solvent businesses from borrowing out of caution while providing liquidity to all who truly needed it, without subsidizing failed institutions.

Instead of following the lessons of Hamilton and Bagehot, however, governments began to offer cheap loans to banks, thereby bailing out insolvent ones and lessening the blow to their creditors. Knowing full well that the lender of last resort will save them if they run into trouble, bankers and investors take bigger risks, making asset bubbles much larger than they would become in the absence of the insurance provided by government bailouts and backstops. Too-big-to-fail doctrine, which promises unlimited funds to very large institutions thought to pose systemic risks, is especially pernicious because it subsidizes the wealthiest at the expense of taxpayers and smaller competitors (Wright 2010).

Stick With Competition, the Rest of the World Is

The incentives people face throughout financial markets and throughout political settings influence their behavior for better or worse. That is, while we can create rules and regulations that encourage risky purchases and entrench special interests, we can also create rules that dissuade such things. Instead of raising the barriers to entry into banking via regulations, like the onerous *de novo* application process, regulators could allow banks to compete across the risk–return spectrum. If consumers bear the consequences of where they deposit idle balances and if financial intermediaries bear the consequences of how they compose their balance sheet, they will more quickly transform liabilities into assets, transfer risk, and alleviate information asymmetry problems. Competition will not always prevent banks from acquiring risk, and it will not prevent the next bubble or financial crisis. It will, however, avoid the many problems caused by governmental regulation, discourage special interests from pursuing their own interests at the expense of the public, and encourage innovation.

Lastly, the increasingly global financial system—driven by improvements in computing and communications technology—also suggests the need for less, rather than more, regulation. Consumers can deposit funds throughout the world with a couple keystrokes and phone taps; banks can perform their role as intermediaries at the same scale. Any regulation a government might want to pursue—as noble as it might seem—can be easily avoided. Regulators cannot readily improve on competitive outcomes.

CHAPTER 13

Central Banking

In many countries and currency unions like the EU, the main financial regulator, the lender of last resort, and the main manager of deposit insurance and interest rates is the central bank. Central banks can provide stability and, perhaps, direct the course of commercial activity. They can also be a source of instability, however, as they distort prices and alter balance sheets.

The Federal Reserve, Born in Crisis, a Product of Government

The power to stabilize and disrupt individual plans and financial markets was not a power people treated lightly. Debates surrounding the creation of the Federal Reserve system—the central bank in the United States—and whether it should have explicit powers to regulate the supply of money began decades prior to its creation (Meltzer 2004; Wood 2008). While such a power could be beneficial if used appropriately to calm financial markets or adjust the money supply to macroeconomic conditions, it could also lead to a concentration of power and wealth that would tend to benefit private, not public, interests. Even if central bankers were angelic, it is not clear they could ever possess sufficient knowledge to intervene in the economy at the right time, or with sufficiently tailored tools, to improve market outcomes.

The unique characteristics of central banks—their ability to intervene in financial markets—highlights the precariousness of their power. Central banks often are the government's bank, which means they can print money or provide loans to the government, they have a monopoly on currency issues, and they have deep ties to the state. The central bank's close relationship to the government provides it a legal legitimacy to intervene in financial markets and pursue the objectives of its leaders instead of the public interest.

Created in 1913, the Federal Reserve is a newcomer relative to the central bank scene. While Britain's central bank, The Bank of England, began operating in the late 17th century, The Bank of Amsterdam began in 1609. Creators of the Federal Reserve were most influenced by America's first two central banks, private institutions both called the Bank of the United States (1791–1811; 1816–1836). Although both institutions were wildly successful, both profitable and effective, Americans remained quite wary of centralized financial power and did not want a central bank with numerous branches. The nation remained on a bimetallic (gold and silver) standard, so the money supply was largely determined exogenously, that is, by market forces, with the Bank of the United States simply serving as a check on state banks and an occasional lender of last resort under Hamilton's/Bagehot's Rule. Those functions, however, could be carried out locally by smaller institutions. The Suffolk Bank, for example, facilitated money exchanges and lending for banks in and around Boston. This bank also mitigated shocks associated with bank runs and panics (Smith, Rolnick, and Weber 2000). Other private clearinghouses served similar functions.

Despite not having a central bank between 1836 and 1914 (when the Federal Reserve began operations), many people perceived problems with the financial system, especially after the panic of 1907. That panic—precipitated by gold and silver flows and interest rate increases initiated by the San Francisco earthquake and the risky investments of a few trust companies that ultimately failed—culminated in runs on other banks and big declines in stock prices and a short but sharp recession. The panic further stimulated a desire to create a larger bank that could provide stability in response to future panics. These problems, the surrounding debates, and federal legislation led to the creation of a wholly new financial institution, that is, The Federal Reserve system (the Fed). Created by the Federal Reserve Act of 1913, the Fed was a compromise between people who wanted the bank to be a source of stability in response to changing interest rates, a source of funds in response to seasonal changes in bank reserves, and a lender of last resort, and people who wanted to place constraints on the bank to avoid it having an overriding influence on banking and financial markets.

Structure Minimizes Dominance, Checks Abuse, and Pursues Goals

The Federal Reserve structure is built on regional and organizational divisions designed to prevent one person or a group of people from using monetary policy and enacting financial rules to pursue private ends. Thus, there are three organizational parts to the Federal Reserve system that seek to disperse the Fed's powers and responsibilities. There are 12 regional districts of the Federal Reserve system, each led by a Federal Reserve Bank. Initially, each district bank had the ability to enact monetary policy for its region, each of which encompasses multiple states. The Board of Governors decides the general course of the bank's policies nationally. Finally, the Federal Open Market Committee rules the Fed's monetary policy, establishing goals for interest rates or money supply growth. Other advisory groups also exist, and technically private member banks, all federally chartered banks and the state-chartered banks that opt to join, own the Fed via their ownership of restricted equity shares in the institution.

Federal Reserve Banks

The Fed's district banks form the conduit between the monetary policy goals selected by the Board of Governors and the Federal Open Market Committee (FOMC) and commercial banks, regular consumers, and day-to-day commercial activity. When monetary policy goals change, the district banks have the responsibility to pursue it using their access to local banks and their respective local economies.

Each of the 12 district banks also have their own checks and balances. As a part of the Federal Reserve system, they are federally chartered and overseen by the Board of Governors; at the same time, they are owned by the local commercial banks in their region. Each bank is managed by a bank president and a group of nine directors, three from regional commercial banks, three from the business community, and three appointed by the Board of Governors to represent the public interest. The six directors representing the public interest, rather than those chosen by the regional banks, select the president. Each president of the 12 district banks serves on the FOMC, which today largely determines national monetary policy.

Federal Open Market Committee

The FOMC was created in 1936 and is comprised of the seven governors on the Board of Governors, the president of the regional bank of New York, and a rotating selection of four of the remaining district bank presidents. The chair of the FOMC also chairs the Board of Governors; moreover, the president of the New York district bank always serves as the vice chair of the FOMC.

This body meets every six weeks and has long focused its attention on the federal funds rate target, or the interest rate banks within the Federal Reserve system use when making overnight loans to each other. The overnight rate is thought to influence nominal market interest rates, the rates that banks charge businesses and individuals. Nominal interest rates of course influence real interest rates, and hence incentives to borrow, via the Fisher effect. The FOMC thus raises its target overnight rate to increase the cost of borrowing to slow economic growth and hence inflation. It lowers the overnight rate when it wants to stimulate economic activity to stave off a recession.

The members of the FOMC and their staff gather information and reports about the economy to assess current economic conditions before deciding whether to increase, decrease, or leave its overnight target as is. The members also debate how to communicate its policy changes because expectations play a large role in financial markets. Because changes made during the Global Financial Crisis decreased the importance of the federal funds rate, such forward guidance has played an increasingly important role in monetary policy, especially if the guidance is viewed as credible, that is, something the Fed will actually do. If, for example, market participants believe future Federal Reserve policy will lower the inflation rate, expected inflation falls, which can help to lower nominal rates.

Board of Governors

This body of the Federal Reserve system is made up of seven people—appointed by the president of the United States and confirmed by the senate—who serve single, staggered 14-year terms. The term limits tend to insulate governors from political pressure, and their staggered terms limit the influence any one governor might have while ensuring that the board is always composed of seasoned veterans as well as new blood. Additional organizational rules include the presidential appointment of the chair and two vice-chairs and a restriction that no more than two governors can come from the same district.

The Board of Governors has the following responsibilities: it sets the reserve requirement, which is now largely a dead letter; approves recommendations regarding the discount rate, the rate at which district banks lend to member banks; and monitor rules regarding consumer credit protection, approve bank mergers, and supervise the management of member banks.

Serving Multiple Masters

With such divisions in place and checks on power, Congress tasks the Federal Reserve with the goal of maintaining a reasonable tradeoff between inflation and employment. Reasonable means different things to different people, but this is the key tension central bankers face. The Fed could allow unemployment to rise to curb inflation, but most would agree an unemployment rate or an inflation rate of, say, 50 percent is unacceptable, so it often must try to intervene in the macroeconomy to prevent such extremes. When it does so, however, it is not subject to a hard and fast rule. Central bankers are bounded in what they can do, but they have leeway to use discretion regarding what they believe is appropriate. The Fed also pursues systemic stability via monitoring and regulating financial markets and acting as a lender of last resort during crises.

As we will see in Chapter 14, the Federal Reserve conducts monetary policy to pursue its main objectives. Members of the FOMC, the Board of Governors, and the chairman of the Fed use available data and analytical models to assess whether monetary policy changes are appropriate, and, if they are, how to implement those changes. For example, if members of the FOMC expect a recession is coming, Federal Reserve policy— given the goals of maintaining full employment—might be to attempt to lower the federal funds rate, which might stimulate economic activity. The idea and hope are that the recession will be shorter and milder because of the change in rates initiated by the deliberations of the FOMC and the actions of the Federal Reserve.

If the Fed lowers the cost of credit to mute a recession, however, it might stimulate inflation. It must always walk a fine line between inducing recession and inflation, which is a difficult task. Sometimes it does so successfully, but sometimes it causes stagflation, to wit inflation and recession simultaneously, as during the Great Inflation in the 1970s. Other times, it causes, or at least does not prevent, periods of low inflation and economic growth, like the Great Moderation of the 1990s and early 2000s.

But Independence Is Rare

Central bank effectiveness depends on its ability to pursue the goals of monetary policy according to economic principles without interference from political pursuits. This stance might seem controversial, especially if you value democratic political institutions. If central banks are independent, it means there is a lot of power—or the potential to alter the course of economic activity at the very least—lying in the hands of a few experts and bureaucrats. Oversight from elected representatives might provide additional checks on central bankers; such oversight can discourage abuse and can encourage the selection of goals and policies desired by the people.

There are good reasons, however, to suggest independence is an essential feature of central banking in a fiat currency system. A central bank that is allowed to hire experts in economics, monetary policy, and data analysis will be better able to analyze economic conditions and implement appropriate responses. However, a central bank that ties itself to the people running government—or a bank that allows political oversight or unrestricted lending to governments—will tend to finance government projects, which can crowd out private commercial activity; it can reward the friends of those in power and special interests; it can enact inappropriate monetary policies; and it might lead to a higher rate of inflation by trying to stimulate the economy just before elections.

Central banks maintain independence when formal rules that facilitate independence, like constitutional or treaty protections, autonomous budgeting, and sundry governance checks and balances, remain in effect because they render central bankers free from the influence of legislatures or executive branch agencies.

Crude indices of central bank independence exist and are negatively correlated with the level and variance of inflation (Alesina and Summers 1993). Multiple measures suggest central banks in Europe and in Asia are the most independent—these are central banks in the Kyrgyz Republic, Latvia, Hungary, Armenia, and Bosnia and Herzegovina; central banks in India, Saudi Arabia, Singapore, and the United States are the least independent (Dincer and Eichengreen 2014). These measures account for rules regarding whether the chief executive is independent, whether the central bank can make its own policy, and whether—and under what conditions—the bank can lend to government.

Importantly, independence can erode if politicians implicitly or explicitly threaten central banks. That is why many commentators decried the Trump administration for its critical stance on Federal Reserve policy. Specifically, Trump and others in his administration lambasted Fed interest rate increases as foolish and detrimental to economic growth. Trump even intimated that he might not reappoint the chairman, the only governor who can serve multiple four-year terms. The Biden administration also threatened the Fed's independence by nominating an individual with no monetary policy experience and a strong ideological agenda. Public calls and threats to appoint partisan appointees can severely undermine the credibility of a central bank, which leaves it a less effective tool of macroeconomic stabilization.

The Federal Reserve faces a more serious—and older—set of problems than the actions of POTUS, a fairly weak grasp on independence. While it maintains an institutional structure that nominally guards against political pressure, such strictures are easily avoided or are counteracted by other incentives people face within the Fed. Given our introduction to public choice economics in Chapter 12, we can see why. Incentives have shaped Federal Reserve structure and policy since its inception. Politicians like Carter Glass from Virginia and Champ Clark from Missouri influenced the Fed system and secured their favored cities for one of the 12 district banks. Missouri is the only state that is home to two of the 12 district banks—in St. Louis and in Kansas City—which was necessary to secure the Fed's charter. Such examples of logrolling pursue private, not public, interests.

Politicians favoring expansionary monetary policy constantly pressure the Federal Reserve. Presidential appointments can encourage the selection of governors who favor expansionary policies, as well as the intimidation of governors who favor contractionary policies. For example, Reagan appointed Manley Johnson to undermine Paul Volcker while he was trying to fight inflation with high interest rates and steep, unpopular recessions. Similarly, Clinton appointed Alan Blinder to undermine Alan Greenspan (Boettke, Salter, and Smith 2021).

The logic of concentrated benefits and dispersed costs also plays a role in the erosion of Federal Reserve independence. Member banks of the Fed often favor policies that benefit member banks. Similarly, people who work for the Fed, banks, and financial regulators benefit from a revolving door, especially as they advance rules to benefit themselves (Boettke, Salter, and Smith 2021).

Not all expertise serves the common good either. A recent study of insider information and announcements of Federal Reserve policy, for example, shows a leaky ship at the New York Fed bank. After analyzing taxicab trips between the New York Federal Reserve district bank and major financial intermediaries in New York, Finer (2018) argues that repeated rides between these locations and similar destinations, prior to major policy announcements, are too suspicious to be random or coincidental. If people working for the Federal Reserve make use of their position and insider information to pursue their own interests, it doesn't merely look bad for the institution. Such activities cast doubt on the ability of experts to pursue the public good.

Other incentives follow from the Fed's bureaucratic, hierarchical structure, which encourages group think and growing budgets with little regard for proper monetary policy, let alone the public good. The Fed employs thousands of economists, analysts, and policy advisers. Moreover, many of these employees face incentives—created by the bureaucracy—to alter their views or face censorship, professional backlash, delayed promotion, or dismissal. Boettke, Salter, and Smith (2021) suggests that the incentives created by the Federal Reserve system encourage central bankers to set aside previously held opinions regarding monetary policy and pursue policies related to the use of discretionary—and often expansionary—monetary policy. Frederic Mishkin—an economist and former member of the Board of Governors—states that "… the most serious problem with the Fed's institutional framework and the way it currently operates is the strong dependence on the preferences, skills, and trustworthiness of the individuals in charge of the central bank" (Mishkin 2009, 54).

The Fed also has a long history of accommodating government spending—or engaging in expansionary monetary policy to finance government spending—which suggests an implicit dependence on political concerns. More pernicious, perhaps, is the higher rate of inflation that inevitably comes with such spending but also a more blurred distinction between monetary and fiscal policy. A key to central bank independence, thus, is a constrained fiscal state, which seems unlikely to return given policy responses to the Great Recession and COVID-19.

An Ever-Growing Balance Sheet

In response to those shocks, the Federal Reserve rapidly expanded its balance sheet and, as Figure 13.1 indicates, it shows little signs of stopping.

This is worrisome as the Fed's independence has waned as its size relative to the financial system has grown. Such expansion indicates a growing role for government and political actors in how money and financial assets are allocated and hence less efficient and riskier financial markets.

Moreover, the Federal Reserve system is dominated by one district bank above all others, the one headquartered near Wall Street. In addition to maintaining 45 percent of the Fed's reserves, the New York Fed is almost wholly responsible for administering the open market operations essential to implementing monetary policy.

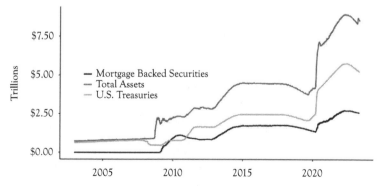

Figure 13.1 Federal Reserve assets, 2002 to 2023

Source: FRED database using fredr.

CHAPTER 14

Monetary Policy, Targets, and Goals

We have a general idea of what central banks do, and while we might not have confidence in their independence, they have confidence in their purpose, their expertise, and in their ability to use monetary policy to influence economic activity. Whether you agree with such goals and/or policies, you should better understand how the tools of monetary policy work and how they influence economic activity.

Central Banks Face a Balancing Act Too

By changing the size and composition of their balance sheets, central banks influence the money supply and cost of credit, thereby affecting economic activity. Like all economic entities, central banks have balance sheets that change as they acquire assets (things owned) and issue liabilities (things owed). Their balance sheets most closely resemble those of commercial banks, with the major exception that in addition to deposits they also issue notes, like Federal Reserve Notes (FRN) in the case of America's central bank. FRN (and other central bank currencies) are the liabilities of their issuers, the Fed (or other central banks), but the assets of the holders. The same holds for reserves, which are simply deposits of commercial banks held by the Fed. Unlike most liabilities, however, the Fed's monetary liabilities (FRN and reserves) are not redeemable for dollars or anything else for that matter. When returned to the Fed, they simply stop existing, in an economic sense anyway. The same would hold true if you received your own IOU for payment of a debt owed you, or a purchase you made.

The Fed's two monetary liabilities allow it to engage in monetary policy. In Chapter 11, we recognized that currency in circulation and bank reserves comprise the monetary base; in this chapter, we develop the link between the monetary base and monetary policy. The Fed uses the tools of monetary policy to change the amount of currency in circulation (FRN plus treasury's fiduciary coins, for example, dimes, quarters, etc., which are *de minimus* in value and hence generally ignored) and bank reserves. As we know from the deposit creation process, such changes ultimately influence the money supply.

Consider an example where the Fed purchases $1,000,000 in Treasury Bills (T-bills as they are called) from a commercial bank. That purchase indicates an acquisition of assets for the Federal Reserve and an increase in the Fed's liabilities, the money it issued to purchase the T-bills. The selling bank, by contrast, exchanged one asset (T-bills), for another, the FRN and/or reserves it received in exchange. Reserves are deposits in the Fed and hence assets to commercial banks, and they are liabilities to the Federal Reserve. Tables 14.1 and 14.2 show the t-accounts for the Fed and a commercial bank, respectively, for a $1,000,000 bond purchase.

Thus, changes in a central bank's balance sheet is a relatively simple way to think about how monetary policy impacts the monetary base and, ultimately, the money supply. Central bank asset purchases cause an expansion in the money supply per the deposit creation process. Central bank asset sales shrink the money supply by removing currency and/or reserves from circulation as the monetary liabilities the central bank issued are returned to it in exchange for the assets it sold. A central bank can alter its balance sheet in multiple ways described next.

Table 14.1 The Fed purchases $1,000,000 in treasuries

Assets	Liabilities
+ $1,000,000 (U.S. Treasuries)	+ $1,000,000 (FRN)

Table 14.2 A commercial bank sells $1,000,000 in Treasuries

Assets	Liabilities
- $1,000,000 (U.S. Treasuries)	
+ $1,000,000 (FRN)	

Open Market Operations Have the Spotlight

Open market operations (OMO) entail the purchase or sale of assets by a central bank. Central bankers long employed OMO because they can be tailored and timed with precision in an attempt to meet monetary policy goals. If FOMC members fear a decline in economic activity, they can stimulate the economy by purchasing treasury bonds and other securities, thus increasing the money supply and likely lowering interest rates. They can direct the FRBNY, the Federal Reserve bank charged with conducting OMO, to buy as many or as few treasuries or other assets as they believe necessary to stave off the impending recession in an open market purchase (OMP). If FOMC members believe that they went too far, risking inflation or a financial bubble, they can easily reverse course by ordering the FRBNY to sell assets.

Discount Lending Is an Important Sideshow

Discount lending is another monetary policy tool that allows the Federal Reserve to act as a lender of last resort to individual banks facing temporary distress. When commercial banks that seem fundamentally sound face runs on their deposits or other liabilities, the Federal Reserve can lend to them even if other commercial banks are hesitant to lend, usually due to asymmetric information. Despite being a bank of sorts, the Federal Reserve does not want to be in the lending business unless it has to be, so it generally increases the discount rate, the rate it charges banks that want to borrow from it, along with other policy rates to dissuade them from using the Fed's discount window (an anachronistic term from the old days of banking) unless absolutely necessary. It always hinted that banks that borrowed from it would face increased regulatory scrutiny too. Tables 14.3 and 14.4 show how a $50 million loan from the Fed to a commercial bank influences their respective balance sheets.

Table 14.3 The Fed lends $50,000,000

Assets	Liabilities
+ $50,000,000 (discount loan)	+ $50,000,000 (FRN)

Table 14.4 A commercial bank borrows $50,000,000

Assets	Liabilities
+ $50,000,000 (FRN)	+ $50,000,000 (discount loan)

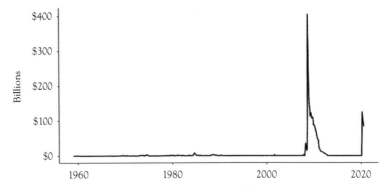

Figure 14.1 Discount lending to commercial banks, 1959 to 2020

Source: FRED database using fredr.

Moreover, the discount window does not lend itself to an activist monetary policy; commercial banks might not borrow when the Fed wants to increase the money supply and might repay sooner than desirable. Given the stigma associated with borrowing from the Fed, banks rarely do so. Figure 14.1 shows the amount of discount lending, which highlights how little it is used under normal circumstances and how it is used during times of financial stress and uncertainty, like the financial crisis of 2007 to 2009 and the COVID-19 pandemic.

Reserves Can Rise and Fall

Another traditional tool of monetary policy entails changing the required reserve ratio, or in other words, the reserves banks must hold in their vault (FRN) or with the Fed (reserves). The Fed could influence the money supply by increasing or decreasing the percentage of checkable deposits it requires banks to hold in reserve. Changes in this requirement, while it remained a binding constraint on banks, influenced the deposit creation process. When bankers were legally required to hold additional reserves, fewer dollars were available to lend, slowing deposit creation by decreasing the money multiplier. Decreasing the requirement allowed bankers to hold fewer dollars in reserves, leaving them more dollars to lend, which speeds deposit creation by increasing the money multiplier. The tool was so powerful that the Fed rarely employed it and actually induced a recession in 1937 by raising the reserve requirement too much, too soon. Today, the tool remains unused as it has lost most of its power due to early FinTech innovations, like so-called sweep accounts, that allow banks to reduce their checkable deposits instead of increasing their reserves.

The Market for Federal Funds Sets the Stage

The Fed's primary monetary policy tool—and the one most frequently discussed in the news—is the target federal funds rate, a range of interest rates that tend to clear the overnight bank-to-bank lending market. When the Fed sets a target rate range, it signals its stance on monetary policy. Higher targets indicate contractionary policies; lower targets indicate expansionary policies. Like any other market, the market for overnight bank-to-bank loans follows the logic of supply and demand. For example, if banks are willing to lend more dollars than other banks are willing to borrow, the federal funds rate falls; if banks want to borrow more dollars than other banks are willing to lend, the federal funds rate rises. To keep the market rate within its policy target zone, the FRBNY engages in the appropriate OMO, making OMP (purchases) or OMS (sales) as needed to add or remove reserves from the banking system. While the Fed long conducted monetary policy via OMO, during the Great Recession it began to pay interest on excess reserves to alter its target. Figure 14.2 shows how the federal funds rate has moved over time.

Managing Tradeoffs Gives Direction

Central bankers face several serious tensions or tradeoffs. Most importantly, pursuit of expansionary monetary policies (EMP) will lead to a higher rate of inflation and greater financial market instability. Fending off a recession, by lowering the federal funds target rate and engaging in OMP, creates inflationary pressures.

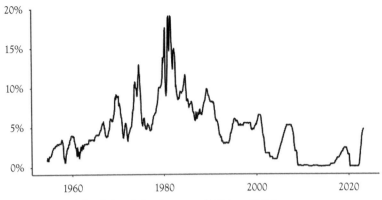

Figure 14.2 The federal funds rate, 1954 to 2023

Source: FRED database using fredr.

Inflation is a problem because it distorts economic decision making and can dampen real economic growth and, more importantly, economic development. Keeping the amount of bank reserves stable will stabilize the rate of inflation, but pursuing that policy means that any change in the demand for reserves—which changes the interest rate—must go unmet. In other words, price level stability comes at the expense of interest rate volatility. Alternatively, keeping interest rates stable comes at the expense of changing the amount of bank reserves, which can lead to a higher rate of inflation. These tensions require central banks to explicitly face such tradeoffs and work toward defining a hierarchy of these goals.

One of the easiest ways for central banks to manage such tradeoffs is to establish, announce, and attempt to consistently pursue a monetary target. Appropriate monetary targets are adjustable, observable, and relevant, characteristics that maintain the discretion of central bankers to alter monetary policy as they deem appropriate to respond to crises.

Interest rate targets, like the federal funds rate, gives central bankers discretion. Such rates are observable, and hence provide transparency and accountability. Figure 14.3 shows how the federal funds rate target—comprised of an upper and lower bound—has changed since the global financial crisis.

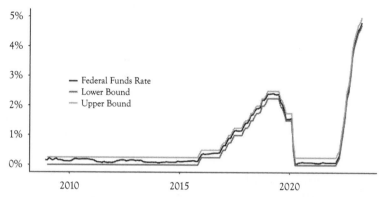

Figure 14.3 The federal funds rate and target range, 2009 to 2023

Source: FRED database using fredr.

The Taylor Rule Is a Guide

While there isn't a book of directions—or a fortune teller—to tell members of the FOMC where to set the federal funds target range, monetary economists like John Taylor have proffered rules they might follow to balance the goals of economic growth and price level stability. The Taylor rule and all other rules are ultimately normative, in that they make value judgments about the relative importance of growth and inflation, but they make them explicit, precise, and transparent.

The Taylor rule, for example, says that the target federal funds rate *ff* should (there's the normative part) rise along with the real, short-term interest rate i_r, the current inflation rate π, and a weighted sum of the inflation gap and the output gap where the inflation gap is the difference between the current rate of inflation and the target rate of inflation, and the output gap is the difference between the current rate of output and the potential rate of output. More formally:

$$ff^* = i_r + \pi + \frac{1}{2}(inflation\ gap + output\ gap)$$

In the following example, note the relatively high rate of inflation and an economy that is producing slightly above its potential. Both of these factors suggest it would be appropriate to raise the federal funds rate following the Taylor rule. If the real, short-term interest rate is 3 percent, the current rate of inflation is 7 percent (where the central bank target rate of inflation is 2 percent), and the current rate of output is 4 percent (where the potential output is 3 percent), the target federal funds rate should equal 13 percent.

The federal funds rate set by the Taylor rule implies a strong reaction to increases in the rate of inflation relative to changes in output. That is, because inflation enters into the rule twice—once on its own and once in the weighted sum—changes in inflation play a larger role in driving changes in the federal funds rate. This gives the Taylor rule a neat thermostat-like feature; the federal funds target rate should rise with inflation but at a faster rate than the rate of inflation and *vice-versa*. By raising rates, it becomes more expensive to borrow, which limits business investment and consumption and puts downward pressure on prices.

Do members of the FOMC follow the Taylor rule? Although the actual federal funds rate sometimes follows the rate suggested by the Taylor rule, members of the FOMC do not clearly follow it. Figure 14.4 shows how changes in the federal funds rate differ from the rate suggested by the Taylor rule. Some of the difference, though, may stem from the assumptions used to construct the Taylor rule measurement. Figure 14.4 assumes both the inflation target and the real interest rate are 2 percent.

When the Taylor rule suggests rates should rise, they do, but with a delay. Rates also fall when the Taylor rules suggests they should fall, but again with a delay. It appears that FOMC members fear moving too quickly, perhaps because macroeconomic data can move stochastically

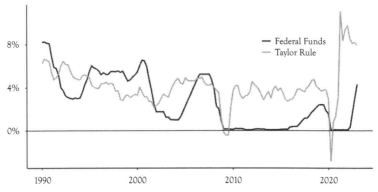

Taylor Rule assuming a 2% target rate of inflation and a 2% short-term real interest rate

Figure 14.4 Federal funds rate versus the Taylor rule, 1990 to 2023

Source: FRED database using fredr.

and are subject to later revision. Or perhaps FOMC members wait so that the special interests that have captured the Fed can profit from the delay.

But Not a Stand-In for Discretion

Some policy pundits have suggested simply adopting something like the Taylor rule to replace the Fed's discretionary powers, which can be corrupted by political and commercial influences. But during crises or unexpected changes in economic conditions—not captured by changes in inflation or in output—discretion might be important, rule skeptics argue. In response to the COVID-19 pandemic, for example, the Fed lowered the federal funds rate to near zero, where it remained well into 2022, even as inflation soared to 40-year highs. The Taylor rule, however, would not have lowered the federal funds rate so drastically. The economy might not have recovered as quickly as it did from government-imposed lockdowns, but then again, inflationary pressures would not have built so much. Maybe the best thing is to run the Fed like an airplane, with auto-pilot on most of the time but a couple of experienced pilots in the cabin just in case a rule cannot be implemented.

Unconventional Times Call for Unconventional Measures

OMO, discount lending, and required reserves are conventional monetary policy tools. While such tools often produce a low, steady rate of inflation, full employment, and a stable financial system, they face limits, especially the zero-lower bound. Between October 2008 and May 2017 and between April 2020 and February 2022, the federal funds rate remained near zero consistently. While some nominal interest rates have dipped a little below zero due to deflation expectations, negative overnight rates make no economic sense, so monetary policy makers cannot drive them much below zero for long enough to matter.

How then can they engage in expansionary monetary policy (EMP)? By engaging in unconventional monetary policy, especially quantitative easing (QE), or when central banks purchase assets to support prices without trying to lower the federal funds rate. Other unconventional monetary policy tools include forward guidance and paying interest on excess reserves.

Quantitative Easing and Targeted Asset Relief Programs

QE refers to the Fed's purchase of assets beyond the point at which such purchases influence the federal funds rate. Such purchases do not influence current rates because they are already too low, but they do increase the money supply and thus inflation expectations, thus lowering real interest rates via the Fisher equation. Figure 13.1 and the spikes in assets between 2008 and 2015—and then again in 2020—illustrate recent examples of QE.

The Fed can also use QE to bolster specific asset markets. Instead of purchasing treasuries and related securities, members of the FOMC can order the FRBNY to purchase derivatives, mortgages, and even real estate equities. Such purchases can prevent the prices of those assets from collapsing, which could trigger bankruptcies and distress banks or other financial institutions. For example, during the Financial Crisis of 2007 to 2009—and throughout the following years—the Fed acquired $1.8 trillion in mortgage-backed securities. These purchases took those relatively risky assets off the balance sheets of commercial banks, which bolstered mortgage prices and the perceived health of commercial banks.

Forward Guidance

Forward guidance follows the logic of the Fisher equation, seeking to influence long-term real interest rates by manipulating inflation expectations. By credibly committing to a particular federal funds rate in the future, for example, increasing its federal funds target rate next year, the Fed can decrease current inflation expectations, lowering current nominal rates and thereby encouraging increased spending. Generally following rules like the Taylor rule can help to provide the credibility the central bank needs for forward guidance to be effective.

Interest on Excess Reserves

Traditionally, the Fed did not pay interest on required reserves, or any excess reserves that banks might choose to hold for prudential reasons.

Once sweep accounts rendered required reserves largely moot, the Fed, following the lead of other central banks, began in 2008 to entice banks to hold reserves by paying interest on them. By offering a higher rate (called the IOER), the Fed encourages banks to lend to it instead of to other banks or nonbank borrowers. By inducing banks not to lend as much as they otherwise would, the Fed can increase the supply of reserves via OMO and QE while easing inflationary pressures. To see this, recall the money multiplier discussed in Chapter 11. As excess reserves rise—because the Fed pays banks to increase excess reserves—the M1 multiplier falls, curtailing the deposit creation process. When the Fed engaged in multiple bouts of QE during the 2010s, it did not lead to consistently higher rates of inflation because the Fed also raised the interest rate on excess reserves.

Transmission Mechanisms Expand the Scope of Monetary Policy

Conventional tools are more powerful, however, once we recognize that changes in interest rates have diverse, rippling effects on individuals and financial intermediaries. EMP—to encourage investment and bolster aggregate output—does not merely lower the cost of investment via a lower interest rate. EMP also lowers the return on domestic assets, which lowers the demand for domestic assets and for USD—a topic we will cover shortly in Chapter 15. Thus, EMP increases net exports and aggregate output via dollar depreciation. These two effects are traditional channels—also known as transmission mechanisms—of monetary policy. These channels are theoretically relevant, but people and firms don't often base consumption and investment decisions on relatively minor changes in interest and exchange rates. There are other channels, however, that exert larger effects.

EMP provides depository institutions with additional reserves, which increases lending and enhances the deposit creation process. As the central bank exchanges securities for currency, banks have additional reserves and fewer revenue-earning assets. Banks tend to lend more after such policies, which enhances the deposit creation process. This effect is the bank-lending channel, which is especially relevant for individuals and firms that rely on banks for loans, credit, and capital—as opposed to firms that can issue stocks and bonds. As important as we think banks are at resolving information asymmetry problems and transforming liabilities and assets, they become an important channel of monetary policy.

Relatedly, the balance sheets, liquidity, and net worth of individuals, households, banks, and other financial intermediaries rise with EMP. These effects are called balance sheet and net worth channels. As short-term interest rates fall, asset prices tend to rise, and the cost of servicing debt falls. These changes, thus, tend to increase economic activity as they expand balance sheets and net worth. Moreover, banks will be more likely to lend as individuals and firms seem more creditworthy.

Particular assets like stocks and real estate might be particularly susceptible to changing monetary policy. EMP tends to increase the present value of such assets as it increases the expected value of future dividends. Similarly, mortgage rates tend to fall. EMP, thus, spurs higher asset prices as people can develop expectations of growth and higher future stock and real estate prices. As people and firms earn capital gains on these assets, their income, consumption, and investment rise.

Conventional and unconventional monetary policies—combined with these channels—suggest central banks influence individuals and financial intermediaries in many ways. Central banks might still face a zero-lower bound, where such policies are less effective, but they have other channels to explore and analyze.

CHAPTER 15

International Monetary Policy

Central bankers must consider the effects of foreign financial markets and monetary policies on their domestic economies, no matter how large. This interdependence stems from the globalization of commodities and financial markets, and that economic entities often buy and sell assets denominated in various currencies. Exchange rates become important drivers of the supply and demand for many financial instruments and other internationally traded goods, which can influence the domestic money supply. Thus, foreign exchange rates become an additional monetary policy variable for many central banks.

Countries vary in how large their import and export sectors are as a share of their overall economy. Whereas imports and exports comprise a relatively small share of GDP in the United States—see Figure 15.1—many other countries are more dependent on foreign trade. Their economic welfare depends even more on the drivers of exchange rates and the ability of central banks to influence those rates.

Exchange Rates and Foreign Exchange Markets Are Still Important

To clarify how central banks might influence exchange rates, let's review some of the core concepts discussed in Chapter 8. These concepts focus on the long- and short-run determinants of exchange rates.

In the Long Run

The law of one price suggests identical goods will have the same price once we account for transportation and other transaction costs. The price of the same good in Chicago, New York, Memphis, and Houston differs only by transportation and other transaction costs like taxes. If they

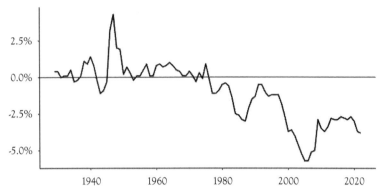

Figure 15.1 Net exports as a share of U.S. GDP, 1929 to 2021

Source: FRED database using fredr.

varied by more than that, people would buy the good where it was cheapest, transport it to where it was dearest, and pocket the difference. That would drive up the price in the cheap market and drive it down in the dear market until the arbitrage opportunity disappeared. The same logic applies to prices internationally. We expect the same goods to have similar prices throughout the world, except for differences in transportation and other transaction costs. It is just more difficult to tell when prices are denominated in different units of account.

The law of one price—and purchasing power parity, which extends the law to all goods—implies that differences in the rate of inflation between countries drive long-run changes in exchange rates. Saying that the money price of goods has increased (inflation) is the same as saying that the price of money has decreased (depreciation). That means that a currency that has experienced lower inflation will be able, all else equal, to buy more units of a currency that has experienced higher inflation. Imagine if the inflation rate in the United States rises relative to the inflation rate in the United Kingdom. The British pound will appreciate, which is to say buy more dollars. In other words, it takes more U.S. dollars to purchase British pounds, just as it takes more dollars to buy gasoline or bread.

And in the Short Run

Short-run determinants of exchange rates also follow the logic of supply and demand. Any factor that influences the demand and supply of

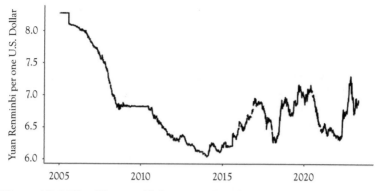

Figure 15.2 The Chinese–U.S. nominal exchange rate, 2005 to 2023

Source: FRED database using fredr.

a currency, including expectations, will influence its exchange rate. For example, the demand for dollars rises when people want to buy more goods from the United States but also when people want to buy more U.S. goods in the future. Either way, *ceteris paribus*, the dollar will appreciate relative to other currencies. Similarly, if Americans want to purchase more goods from Japan, this will lead to an increase in the supply of dollars, a rise in the demand for Japanese yen, and hence, an appreciation of Japanese yen vis-à-vis the dollar.

In a world where goods are mobile and capital controls weak—where investment dollars and physical capital are free to move across borders—exchange rates fluctuate constantly due to changes in expected interest and inflation rate differentials. For example, Figure 15.2 shows that the daily Chinese yuan renminbi to the U.S. dollar exchange rate became much more volatile after China stopped trying to peg the dollar value of the yuan.

When investors have a high degree of capital mobility, we expect they will purchase assets with higher expected returns, controlling for risk. Consider an initial situation where American investors can purchase treasuries from the United States or from Japan.[1] Investors will tend to

---

[1] Chinese bonds might be considered, but they are relatively scarce as there are fewer investment opportunities overall, and such bonds are risky relative to debt issued by the U.S. or Japanese governments.

purchase Japanese treasury bonds, rather than U.S. treasuries, when the expected return on Japanese bonds is higher. If the expected return on Japanese bonds is higher, we will see an increase in the demand for those bonds. This means that demand for dollars will fall and the supply will rise as American investors substitute their currency holdings for Japanese bonds. As a result, dollars depreciate.

Notice a deeper implication when capital markets have a high degree of mobility. That is, there is another change after dollar depreciation. As people increase the demand for Japanese bonds, the price of those bonds rises (its yield falls). This change means that the expected return on Japanese bonds falls, which brings the expected return on both American and Japanese bonds to equality. A higher degree of capital mobility also means that interest rates will tend toward equality across countries.

Central Bankers Buy and Sell Foreign Assets Too

The long- and short-run drivers of exchange rates complicate policy for central bankers. If central bankers want a stable exchange rate—to stabilize price expectations for import/export firms or to encourage domestic manufacturers—they must be prepared to intervene in the foreign exchange market. The central bank must be prepared to counter changes in domestic and foreign inflation and interest rates as well as expectations of future changes.

One of the primary ways a central bank can influence exchange rates is through the purchase or sale of foreign assets denominated in foreign currencies. Imagine the Fed wants to maintain an exchange rate with China at a particular rate, or within a range, say between 6 and 7 yuan per dollar. If the current rate falls below the lower bound of 6 yuan per dollar—the dollar has depreciated relative to yuan—the Fed could sell Chinese yuan in exchange for dollars, which would shrink the Federal Reserve's balance sheet like any other open market sale. The Fed's sale tends to raise domestic interest rates, especially when reserves are relatively scarce, which raises the yield and expected return on U.S. treasuries. As the demand for U.S. treasuries increases and dollars appreciate, the yuan–dollar exchange rate rises back to the desired level.

Whereas the outright purchase and sale of foreign assets influences exchange rates, central banks might want to alter the composition of their balance sheet to influence asset prices without altering exchange rates. That is, they might want to substitute toward bonds and securities from a particular country or toward a particular kind of asset. Central banks can offset their purchase or sale of foreign assets with a corresponding purchase or sale of domestic assets. For example, to *sterilize* the sale of Chinese bonds in the preceding example, the Fed would purchase U.S. treasuries; these two policies offset each other by influencing domestic interest rates in opposing ways.

Central Bankers Still Face Tradeoffs

The preceding discussion implicitly raises three goals of international monetary policy a central bank might want to pursue, namely capital mobility, the use of discretionary monetary policy to influence domestic interest rates, and the use of monetary policy to influence exchange rates. Capital mobility refers to the ability of loanable funds and financial assets to move across borders and to the expectations people have of making international investments. Central banks might want to encourage this mobility because it allows economic entities and financial intermediaries to more cheaply acquire investment portfolios that meet their desired amount of liquidity and risk. Moreover, capital mobility thickens financial markets with many buyers and sellers. Liquidity enhances market competition and reduces the cost of capital. Discretionary monetary policy allows a central bank to respond to crises, to be a lender of last resort, and to dampen shocks to financial markets. Finally, a central bank might want to restrict foreign exchange markets to stabilize the domestic import/export industry. That is, a stable or fixed exchange rate creates expectations about future prices, which helps firms to engage in economic calculation.

There are benefits and costs to each of those goals, and no country can pursue all three simultaneously. This three-way tradeoff—known as the trilemma of international trade or the impossible trinity—means central banks must choose two of these goals and jettison the third. Combinations of goals, known as monetary regimes, possess a unique set of benefits and costs. To summarize the main tradeoffs:

- A country with a fixed exchange rate and capital mobility cannot have discretionary monetary policy because it will not be able to affect domestic interest and inflation rates while maintaining exchange rate stability as capital will flow freely in or out.
- A country with discretionary monetary policy and a fixed exchange rate must impose capital controls because central banks cannot allow markets to upend its efforts to maintain exchange rate stability while it influences domestic interest and inflation rates.
- A country with capital mobility and discretionary monetary policy cannot impose fixed exchange rates because exchange rates will fluctuate as capital flows internationally, and the central bank prioritizes domestic interest and inflation rates.

We will see that the kind of monetary regime a country chooses depends on what policy makers and central bankers value. Those are normative concerns, but we can parse them out to see their costs and benefits. Let's walk through each pairing.

Fixed Exchange Rate and Capital Mobility

In this scenario, central bankers want to fix exchange rates, and they want to ensure free-flowing capital markets. These goals mean, however, that their hands are tied. That is, any change in the interest rate—and, thus, any change in yield and expected return—will alter people's willingness to keep their investments in that country. If a central bank were to engage in expansionary policies, for example, yields would fall and people would move their investments into areas with higher returns.

Central banks are unnecessary in such a monetary regime, the prime example of which was the gold standard prior to the First World War. Some nations had private central banks that operated mainly as lenders of last resort and regulators in that period, and that adopted discretionary monetary policies during wars by *going off gold*, that is, allowing exchange rates to fluctuate. When currencies are defined as a unit of gold, the exchange rate between them is fixed, and capital mobility is necessary to ensure the international flow of gold that allows the system to self-regulate. If 1 ounce of gold equals $20.00 and 1 ounce of gold equals about £4, we expect an exchange rate of about $5 per £1. Between 1880 and 1910—the classical gold standard period—the dollar-sterling exchange rate indeed ranged between 4.80 and 4.90.

To help explain this stability, note that substantial fluctuations in exchange rates are quickly whittled away by arbitrageurs willing to settle their accounts in gold instead of dollars or pounds. When people sell gold for dollars, it increases the supply of dollars, thus lowering the dollar's purchasing power. Weaker dollars will decrease U.S. imports by making foreign goods more expensive in dollar terms and increase U.S. exports by making U.S. goods cheaper to foreign buyers. An influx of gold will ensue, which restores equilibrium. Ultimately, then, market forces will drive exchange rates back toward the par level implied by the gold value of the dollar and the pound. A gold standard, thus, leaves little scope for discretionary monetary policy, as economic entities would adjust their gold balances in response.

Discretionary Monetary Policy and a Fixed Exchange Rate

If a central bank wants to maintain discretionary monetary policy and impose a fixed exchange rate, it must give up capital mobility by imposing capital controls. When exchange rates are fixed, central banks have to maintain a large amount of foreign currency assets (or precious metals under a gold exchange standard like Bretton Woods). Combined with any changes in domestic interest rates—due to the central bank's domestic monetary policy—the expected return on domestic assets will surely change. This means that the fixed exchange rate and changes in interest rates can incentivize capital flight, the withdrawal of investment from a country. That can diminish economic activity and leave a central bank with less ability to influence interest rates.

So, a central bank can pursue discretionary monetary policy and a fixed exchange rate only if it is willing to impose substantial, binding capital controls. If each dollar earned from buying and selling assets faced a tax of 100 percent, or if it were illegal to buy or sell foreign assets, such investments will be less profitable and speculative attacks improbable, if not impossible. As a result, a central bank can maintain discretionary monetary policy and a fixed exchange rate, which allows it to influence both domestic interest rates and exchange rates. The downside, of course, is that capital controls might encourage people, their dollars, and other assets to leave the country entirely or to place assets in less restrictive areas.

The Bretton Woods System—the post-Second World War monetary system that mandated the use of U.S. dollars as a world reserve currency—was a monetary regime that allowed countries to have discretionary monetary policy while fixing exchange rates. This system stipulated that each national currency was fixed to the U.S. dollar, forcing foreign central banks in the system to hold large reserves of U.S. dollars and to impose strict capital controls. Otherwise, people would have expected their respective central banks to devalue, and there would be consistent profit opportunities. While the system functioned in name between 1944 and 1971, it became increasingly difficult to maintain as financial markets grew and became more complex and as early FinTech rendered it easier to avoid capital controls.

Capital Mobility and Discretionary Monetary Policy

In the 1970s, the United States became one of many countries to jettison fixed exchange rates (the Bretton Woods gold-exchange system) and discretionary monetary policy in favor of allowing capital mobility while maintaining discretionary monetary policy. Given investors and their dollars are free to seek returns in and out of the country and the Federal Reserve is free to influence short-term rates, it would be impossible for the Fed to maintain a fixed exchange rate. As a result, it leaves foreign exchange rates free to fluctuate according to supply and demand. If the Fed used monetary policy to maintain a fixed exchange rate—which it would do through the purchase and sale of foreign assets—it could not conduct OMO to hit domestic interest and inflation rates targets. Moreover, foreign and domestic investors would either invest in places with higher returns—which they can do, given capital mobility—or they would exploit the fixed exchange rate created by the Fed. Either way, the Fed could not achieve all three of its goals simultaneously.

If the Fed announced it was committed to a fixed exchange rate of £1 for every $1, speculative attacks would soon ensue. The Fed would have to hold large sums in pounds; otherwise, it would probably renege on the fixed rate and depreciate dollars. If investors expect an oncoming devaluation of the dollar, they can observe an actionable profit opportunity. Investors would first borrow $1,000,000, for example, and sell those dollars to the Fed for £1,000,000. Then, investors would purchase short-term British treasuries to earn interest until the Fed runs out of British pounds, which would trigger a devaluation. In the event of a devaluation, where £1 might equal $1.50 overnight, investors can sell their British securities for dollars (about $1.5 million), they will pay back the initial loan (plus interest), and pocket the remainder. Assuming the interest rate on the loan and the interest on the securities are similar, the attackers walk away with $500,000. So long as capital can flow unimpeded, central banks with monetary policy discretion cannot commit to a fixed exchange rate because it requires a large amount of foreign reserves.

This kind of exchange rate regime implies interest parity, which refers to how the yields on domestic and foreign assets—measured in the same currency—tend toward equality. Such an outcome is especially likely when investors view these assets as substitutes, they recognize the profit opportunities associated with arbitrage, and capital is mobile. For example, if the dollar return on domestic bonds exceeded the return on foreign bonds—accounting for changes in the value of the dollar and exchange rate risk—investors would eschew foreign bonds, demand dollars, and purchase domestic bonds. These changes would increase the price of domestic bonds, lowering domestic yields. Generally, the interest parity condition states:

$$i = i_f - \frac{\Delta E^e}{E}$$

Where i equals the domestic interest rate, i_f the foreign interest rate, and $\frac{\Delta E^e}{E}$ is the percent change in the exchange rate. The implications of interest parity—consistent with the short-run determinants of exchange rates—are that dollars appreciate with higher domestic interest rates, lower foreign interest rates, and a higher expected value of dollars in the future.

Monetary Regimes Vary

Exchange Rates Float or Are Put in a Vise

In response to the dismantling of Bretton Woods, many nations now rely on a free float or a monetary regime where exchange rates constantly reflect relative changes in the supply and demand for their currency and the currency of other nations. While this allows for greater capital mobility and hence economic freedom, it causes uncertainty in exchange rates. Foreign exchange rate uncertainty imposes costs on importers and exporters in smaller economies—and headaches for their central bankers.

To respond to such problems—to partially allow for a more active central bank—and to provide importers and exporters with better expectations, many central banks adopt a hybrid monetary regime called a *managed float*. The central bank allows the exchange rate to fluctuate but only within a range of exchange rates, like putting rates in a vise and making the grip tighter or looser. The U.S.–China exchange rate example earlier implicitly referred to a managed float. To keep the exchange rate within a range, a central bank announces its target range and uses OMO to ensure that the exchange rate will not rise above or fall below that range for any significant period. The primary feature of that system is that day-to-day fluctuations in exchange rates—that stem from changes in short-run supply and demand—are allowed to happen; this limited freedom facilitates the competitive process in currency markets. At the same time, a managed float facilitates the formation of expectations about future exchange rates, thus reducing costs for importers, exporters, and others engaged in international trade, especially when they have access to foreign exchange derivative markets.

We Can Peg and Mimic Too

We realized that when people want to maintain capital mobility and a fixed exchange rate, their monetary regime must guard itself against speculative attacks. To avoid the consequences of a speculative attack, central banks must credibly commit to all the exchanges implied by a fixed exchange rate; otherwise, speculators would force a devaluation. There are two ways a central bank can maintain such a commitment, by managing the fixed exchange rate via currency boards or by adopting the currency of another country with more stable foreign exchange rates.

Currency boards are an institutional guard against speculative attacks that make a commitment to exchange domestic and foreign currency. They are particularly successful when the parent central bank holds significant amount of foreign reserves, which makes the board a credible source of exchange. By holding foreign reserves, the currency board can manage the currency transactions desired by domestic economic entities. By tying the hands of a central bank, currency boards can help to manage domestic inflation. Figure 15.3 shows, for example, how the Hong Kong–U.S. exchange rate changed after the Hong Kong Monetary Authority began its operations and committed to an exchange rate of 7.8 Hong Kong dollars for every 1 U.S. dollar. The negligible change in the exchange rate indicates a very stable inflation rate.

Argentina's currency board, which began operations in 1991, also shows how well these monetary regimes can curtail rampant inflation. Following a period of hyperinflation, the Argentine currency board helped to lower the inflation rate to single digits in a matter of years—shown in Figure 15.4. Because of fiscal problems, for example, public spending, an appreciating U.S. dollar, and other factors, however, the currency board collapsed in 2001.

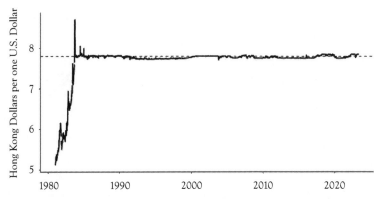

Figure 15.3 The Hong Kong Monetary Authority, 1981 to 2023

Source: FRED database using fredr.

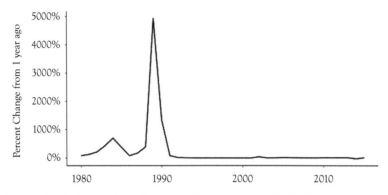

Figure 15.4 Changes in Argentina's consumer price index, 1980 to 2015

Source: FRED database using fredr.

The other way a country can maintain an implicit fixed exchange rate is by merely adopting the currency of another country. Many pick U.S. dollars or euros, or currencies with relatively established central banks. By adopting a more stable currency, a country removes the uncertainty and capriciousness of wild fluctuations in exchange rates. Moreover, adopting a more stable currency avoids the problems related to having a corrupt central bank, which frequently occurs in developing countries. Such a move, generally called *dollarization*, also helps countries to do business anywhere the adopted currency is used. Everything comes with a cost, however. In this case, the adopting country is stuck with the monetary policy of the central bank that controls the currency it adopted. That might mean that interest rates are higher or that inflation is lower than would be optimal for the smaller country. Moreover, obtaining the foreign currency can be difficult. After Ecuador dollarized in 2000, for example, inflation rates there plummeted, but loans proved difficult to obtain.

All the costs and benefits associated with these monetary regimes follow from the impossible trinity or trilemma. Policy makers can pursue any combination of goals they like, but each entails benefits and costs. For example, people in a small developing nation might value stabilizing exchange rates and limiting the discretionary powers of the people who would likely run their central bank. If that is the case, they might want to dollarize or adopt a currency board or a hard peg. Another country with stronger institutional controls might want to retain discretionary monetary policy and capital mobility, which means imposing the costs of a floating exchange rate on its international sector.

CHAPTER 16

Money Demand

When engaging in discretionary monetary policy, central banks face myriad incentives that might clash with the goals of improving economic well-being or stabilizing economic activity. Even if those incentives are appropriately aligned, difficult problems linger. Central bankers can influence the money supply using sundry tools, but they don't always know the consequences of their actions. Such skepticism doesn't mean discretionary monetary policy should be jettisoned for free capital flows or fixed exchange rates, only that caution is in order. Economists, central bankers, and other policy makers rarely have sufficient knowledge about the effects of monetary policy to confidently advocate for tighter or looser monetary policy. Even in a world awash in cheap data, the kind of knowledge policy makers really need is the kind that no one can possess. As Friedrich Hayek (1945) and others argue, what people want can only be known through their actions when faced with real world tradeoffs. This *knowledge problem* is why asymmetric information persists even in our digital age and despite the best efforts of financial institutions and markets to mitigate it. The importance of the knowledge problem for central bankers becomes clear when we consider how changes in the demand for money—something that individuals control—ultimately influences related economic aggregates and alters the efficacy of monetary policy.

An Old, Commonly Accepted Story

To see how complex monetary policy becomes, we should think more carefully about the conditions under which people hold money—a topic that circles back to issues raised in Chapter 2. We know people use money as a means of exchange, a source of liquidity, or the ability to make final payments. Indeed, people converge on commodities and related media of exchange—to discover what we know as money—by substituting goods with lower liquidity for goods with higher liquidity. Moreover, the amount of money people hold depends on the opportunity cost of holding money, which refers to the value of foregone opportunities or the interest rate. The opportunity cost of holding money changes as opportunities to lend and borrow change and as opportunities to acquire assets change. If interest rates rise, the opportunity cost of holding money rises, and people tend to hold less money. As rates fall, the opportunity cost falls, and people tend to hold more money. Changes in the price level also influence our desires to hold money. At low rates of inflation, people are more likely to hold cash, but at higher rates of inflation, they are more likely to hold assets likely to appreciate in nominal terms at least.

One of the oldest theories about money—the quantity theory of money (QTM)—advances the preceding intuitions and develops a more precise relationship between money, interest, prices, and output. The theory dates to 16th-century observations about the effect new world gold strikes had on prices in Europe. Those observations formed into an identity—a true statement about the world like $x = x$—known as the equation of exchange. This identity notes that all of the dollars producers receive must equal all of the dollars consumers spend. In other words, the equation of exchange equates nominal expenditures (the amount of dollars in circulation times how often those dollars are spent) and nominal gross domestic product (the price of goods times the amount of goods). Specifically, the equation of exchange states that

$$Mv = PY,$$

Where M = money supply, v = the velocity of money, P = the price level, and Y = output. This identity is hardly earth shattering or novel; however, it leads to fascinating insights, theories, and testable implications about the relationship between money and prices. Economists are still teasing out the myriad implications of this identity.

Identity as Causal Model

From the equation of exchange, scholars like David Hume, John Locke, Richard Cantillon, Knut Wicksell, Irving Fisher, and others developed the

QTM, which is a set of theories and related propositions showing the relationship between changes in the supply of money and changes in prices. The QTM suggests that the money supply becomes a primary determinant of the price level, especially over long periods of time. Note this is a causal statement: changes in the money supply cause changes in prices.

QTM is a testable hypothesis, so we should examine whether it consistently explains what it purports to explain. Looking at the average money growth and inflation in the United States—shown in Figure 16.1—suggests the QTM holds up fairly well. That is, in years when the average monthly M2 growth trends higher, higher average monthly inflation rates occur.

Figure 16.2 shows a similar graph for Mexico—a country with a larger range of money growth and inflation—which indicates that the QTM still holds.

Another test of a good theory is that it can be extended with subsidiary propositions to account for related observations. In Figures 16.1 and 16.2, for example, outliers seem to clash with the QTM. These observations might simply mean that within the quarter where we observe money growth, its effect on inflation might play out over the next quarter or the next couple years. In any event, note that most of the observations fall below the 45° dashed line. This suggests that for a given amount of money growth, prices rise by a lesser amount. The QTM is poised to explain such

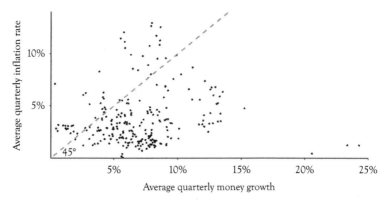

Figure 16.1 Money growth and inflation in the United States, 1960 to 2022

Source: FRED database using fredr.

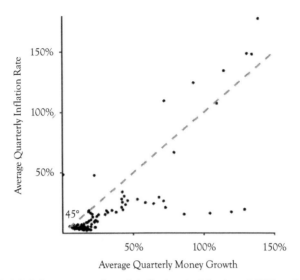

Figure 16.2 Money growth and inflation in Mexico, 1987 to 2022

Source: FRED database using fredr.

phenomenon, perhaps, once we recognize how velocity and output mediate the relationship between money and prices. For example, if money grows by 6 percent and output grows by 5 percent, we should expect the increase in prices to be less than 6 percent. In that case, people spend their additional dollars on a larger set of goods, so we should still expect prices to rise, but by a smaller amount.

A more precise way to examine the relationship between these variables is to note that we are interested in how changes in the variables influence each other. We can rewrite the equation of exchange to account for proportional changes.

$$\%\Delta M + \%\Delta v = \%\Delta P + \%\Delta Y$$

For example, if money grows by 5 percent, velocity increases by 1 percent, and output expands by 1 percent, we should expect an increase in the price level of 5 percent. Overall, the QTM provides a consistent framework to explain the relationship between the money growth and prices, as well as any effects changes in velocity and output might have.

Speaking of changes in velocity and output, we have not fully explained how these factors change, let alone how they influence the relationship between money growth and prices. To start, the equation of exchange suggests that if changes in velocity and prices remain constant, an increase in money growth will equal an increase in output. The real drivers of output, however, depend on a country's economic and political institutions that influence whether people feel secure in their person and property to engage in valuable economic activity. In a 1755 lecture—long before publication of his *An Inquiry into the Nature and Causes of the Wealth of Nations*—Adam Smith effectively said:

> Little else is requisite to carry a state to the highest degree of opulence from the lowest barbarism, but peace, easy taxes, and a tolerable administration of justice; all the rest being brought about by the natural course of things. All governments which thwart this natural course, which force things into another channel, or which endeavor to arrest the progress of society at a particular point, are unnatural, and to support themselves are obliged to be oppressive and tyrannical.

There are many other factors that influence productivity and the wealth of nations, but Smith's message largely rings true today. For our purposes in developing the QTM, however, we simply note that these factors—not related to money—drive long-term changes in productivity. Over shorter, transitional periods, however, changes in productivity can mediate the relationship between money growth and prices.

The velocity of money refers to the speed with which people use money in their transactions or, rather, the number of times a dollar changes hands over some period. The higher the velocity, the more frequently the average dollar is used to buy goods. Much of the debate over the QTM focuses on how quickly velocity changes. Classical monetary economists, including Irving Fisher, believed that velocity changed slowly over long periods of time. Fisher also assumed changes in productivity were negligible. Those assumptions help explain his conclusions regarding the QTM.

Subsequent development in economic thought, however, suggests we should expect velocity to change—especially over shorter periods of time—as the demand for money changes, as income changes, and as financial technology (substitutes for money) changes. Figures 16.3 and 16.4

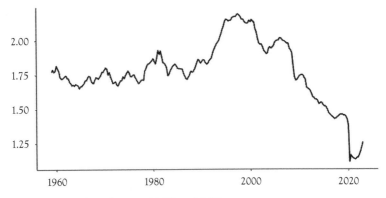

Figure 16.3 M2 velocity, 1959 to 2023

Source: FRED database using fredr.

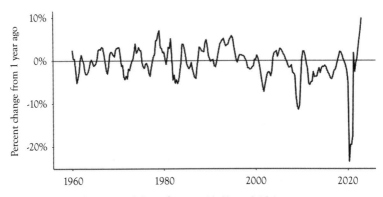

Figure 16.4 Change in M2 velocity, 1959 to 2023

Source: FRED database using fredr.

shows the level and percent change from a year ago of M2 velocity, respectively.

Aside from a few periods, like during the initial stages of the COVID-19 pandemic, long-run trends of M2 velocity seem stable, for example, 1960 to 1990 and 1990 to 2020. Note the typical range in velocity between 1.6 and 2.2, which only falls below 1.6 in 2012. In any event, the level of velocity masks short-run variation. These observations—and what they mean—form the core debate surrounding the effect money growth has on prices. Most scholars agree that the change in velocity over longer periods of time is small, which suggests a greater causal link between money growth and prices over longer periods of time.

There remains, however, considerable debate about how velocity changes over shorter periods of time and why.

Keynes Contributes

The ongoing conversation over what influences changes in velocity is about the conditions under which people are willing to obtain or hold money and bear that opportunity cost. John Maynard Keynes suggested people hold money to make transactions, as a rainy-day precaution, and to speculate. One of the key factors of the demand for money, according to Keynes, was income. As a person's income rises, they tend to purchase more goods, which means they will want to have more money and larger cash balances. More income might also indicate having more in reserve as a rainy-day fund. The interest rate is also an important factor in the demand for money as it indicates one's opportunity cost of money. Similarly, the amount of money held as a precaution falls when it becomes more expensive. As interest rates rise and when the expected future rate rises, people demand fewer dollars and demand more bonds or other assets with a higher return.

These factors—income and the interest rate—form the core of Keynes' approach to the demand for money. Moreover, each of these factors influences velocity. As income rises and people want higher cash balances, velocity falls. That is, the more dollars people want to hold, the fewer times those dollars are exchanged. Similarly, the demand for money rises as the opportunity cost falls, which indicates a lower velocity. Using the difference between the yields on three-month treasuries and the interest rate bearing components of M2 as a measure of the opportunity cost of money, Figure 16.5 shows how the opportunity cost of money influences M2 velocity (measured in terms of percent change from one year ago).

Friedman Contributes Too

As useful as Keynes' ideas about the demand for money are, Milton Friedman developed them further. Friedman viewed money and cash balances as assets people hope to maintain over a long period of time, just like any other asset. This perspective suggests that people alter their

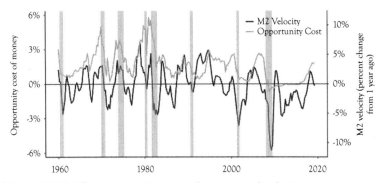

Figure 16.5 *The opportunity cost of money and velocity*

Source: FRED database using fredr.

investments and their demand for money to maintain a similar purchasing power over a long period of time. Multiple predictions follow from Friedman's approach. First, we should expect the demand for money to rise as people expect higher permanent incomes. As people expect to have more income in the future and for longer periods of time, they expect to spend more, which requires additional purchasing power. Thus, real cash balances should increase with additional permanent income. Second, we should expect the demand for money to rise as the opportunity cost of holding cash balances falls. This condition suggests that the expected return on bonds, stocks, and other noncash assets has an inverse relationship with the demand for money. This condition also means that the demand for money falls when the expected inflation rate rises because the expected return on goods like land, gold, and even groceries rises, whereas the return on money decreases with its expected decline in purchasing power.

Friedman's perspective on the QTM is more realistic than Keynes's and other predecessors because it accounts for multiple assets, recognizes that money has a relative return that can change, and suggests that interest rates have a negligible influence, given those rates influence the return on assets and money in opposite directions. Indeed, changes in interest rates rarely affected the demand for money and velocity prior to the 1970s. Throughout the latter part of the 20th century, however, it became cheaper and easier to transfer money between varying states of liquidity. Electronic funds transfer, for example, meant people felt less need to hold significant cash balances in their wallets or even with their banks. Similarly, financial innovations like money market mutual funds became more popular, which provided higher returns than simple checking accounts but also similar liquidity. Such innovations also decrease the demand for money and continue to weaken the tight link between interest and the demand for money Friedman's theory suggests.

Yet Another Constraint Monetary Policy Faces

Given the relationship between money, velocity, prices, and output, we can clarify one of the more difficult problems central bankers face. Over longer periods of time, changes in money growth clearly influence prices. Over shorter periods of time—the timeframe most central bankers are concerned with to stabilize economic activity—money growth is less closely connected to changes in prices. This short-run relationship means that changes in the demand for money—if unaccounted for—can render monetary policy ineffective at best and economically disruptive at worst.

Imagine if the Fed expanded the money supply to fend off a future recession, but it wasn't aware of a decrease in the demand for money. As demand falls, velocity rises. The change in velocity suggests any money growth will have a larger effect on prices (assuming constant output). Instead of thwarting recession, the Fed might inadvertently touch off a bout of inflation.

And Another Lesson Learned From the Great Depression

As we analyze monetary history and consider future monetary policies, changes in the demand for money should take center stage. Notice how the demand for money changed during the Great Depression. Figure 16.6 shows that the annual money velocity decreased by 13 percent (relative to the previous year) in 1931.

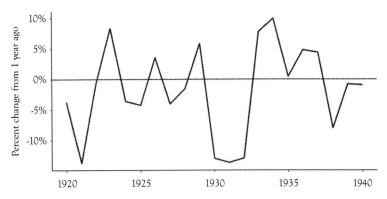

Figure 16.6 The velocity of U.S. money stock, 1920 to 1940

Source: FRED database using fredr.

Intuitively, the decline in velocity after 1929 suggests that people demand higher cash balances as they spend less and save more. This setting clashes, however, with Federal Reserve policy, namely efforts to increase interest rates in 1928, 1931, 1932, and 1936 to 1937. Just when people demanded more money, the Fed used its tools to contract the money supply and limit the deposit creation process.

It Applies to the Great Recession Too

In response to the financial crisis of 2007 to 2009, it seems that the Federal Reserve paid more attention to the demand for money.

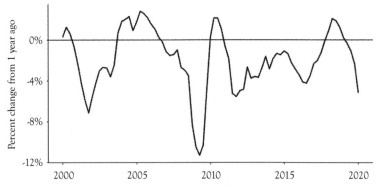

Figure 16.7 Change in M2 velocity, 2000 to 2020

Source: FRED database using fredr.

Figure 16.7 shows the decline in velocity (11 percent) in 2009 relative to the previous year.

Throughout the crisis, especially after August 2008, the Fed lowered rates consistently and kept them near zero until the end of 2016—when rates rose above 0.5 percent. These policies tended to complement, rather than counter, the desires people had regarding money.

CHAPTER 17

Monetary Policy for Tomorrow

In light of all the financial instruments and financial markets people have developed to improve their lives, the relatively minor periods where markets go astray, the normative values people have regarding expansionary monetary policy, and the ever-expanding scope of monetary policy, it remains unclear how monetary policy should be conducted. Previous textbooks on money and banking, for example, distinguish between conventional and unconventional monetary policy, but the unconventional tools like forward guidance and quantitative easing are becoming old hat. Moreover, central bankers maintain inflation and full employment targets, but it is increasingly unclear whether central bankers can achieve either of those outcomes, much less both.

Stabilizing Aggregate Outcomes Is Possible

Central bankers can adjust monetary policy to influence inflation rates and full employment, but this does not mean they control inflation, employment, and output. The real-world effect of monetary policy depends on the decisions of individuals, banks and other financial intermediaries, and politicians and bureaucrats. Central bankers can try to influence those decisions, but they do not control them. People remain free to make choices about consumption and investment, and politicians and bureaucrats make decisions that influence tax rates and public spending. Collectively, those decisions might mean that monetary policy does more harm than good, that is, reducing important macroeconomic outcomes like aggregate output.

Central bankers can enact monetary policy in response to a slew of real shocks, or unexpected events, like natural disasters, pandemics, and wars, that temporarily influence production and economic activity. Wars destroy lives and raise production costs, and decrease output, especially on consumption goods. Changes in economic and political institutions also cause real shocks in positive and negative ways.

Monetary policy might counter these effects because many economic decisions are sensitive to changes in real interest rates. As real interest rates fall, people become more interested in borrowing to purchase cars and homes; businesses also become more interested in physical investment, for example, replacing equipment, acquiring new buildings, and generally expanding operations. Falling real interest therefore tends to increase output.

Note too that changes in domestic monetary policy can change exchange rates, as we discussed in Chapter 8, which also influences aggregate outcomes. As nominal interest rates change in one country (relative to another), open capital markets and the law of one price suggests that exchange rates also will change. Economic entities tend to purchase financial securities in countries with higher interest rates and hence higher expected returns. If, all else equal, rates rise in the United Kingdom, for example, the demand for British financial assets rises, increasing demand for British pounds and hence the appreciation of British pounds vis-à-vis other currencies, like U.S. dollars. This, in turn, leads to a rise in exports (goods from the United States to Britain) and a fall in imports (goods from Britain to the United States) because imports become more expensive and exports cheaper. Thus, British aggregate output rises as net exports—the difference between exports and imports—rise.

Policy makers make decisions that influence aggregate outcomes, albeit these are decisions based on their own interests—to serve narrow constituencies, special interests, or their bureaucratic bosses. Decisions to initiate a war, to increase employment, to provide health care, and so on, all spend public funds, which eventually increases aggregate output or causes inflation.

Businesses also make decisions that influence output. If producers expect a higher rate of inflation in the future, they will tend to increase current production, hoping, while inputs are relatively cheap, to build inventory that can be sold at higher prices in the future. Moreover, any factor that influences the cost of production, for example, changes in the price of oil, labor, or the costs of other inputs, changes the amount of goods firms want to produce. If the price of oil rises, for example, firms will tend to cut back production.

When current and expected inflation rates differ, this also influences decisions to produce and to work. Thus, there is another thermostat-like feature—recall our discussion of the Taylor rule—as firms, workers, and consumers will adjust wages and prices to offset the difference between current and expected inflation. An unexpected rise in the price of oil, for example, raises the current price level above the expected price level; however, producers will eventually increase production as they adjust to a lower expected rate of inflation.

Central bankers must account for these effects, as well as differences in individual time preferences and individual decisions to lend and borrow. When people increase their rate of savings, the supply of loanable funds rises and, all else equal, interest rates decrease. Monetary policy makers should note such changes to avoid countering changes that improve well-being or exacerbating changes that erode well-being. For instance, expansionary monetary policy might be inappropriate when time preferences fall, as it would be more likely to lead to a higher rate of inflation when supercharged by increased savings.

These factors indicate a broad scope wherein central bankers might want to use their tools to increase or decrease interest rates, which can stabilize economic activity. For example, the Fed can lower interest rates in response to falling desires to consume. The Fed could also raise interest rates when governments spend or borrow to offset higher rates of inflation. Engaging in expansionary monetary policy might be inappropriate when the federal government passes a substantial spending bill because both would tend to increase the money supply and can lead to a higher rate of inflation.

Monetary Policy Is Complex

While monetary policy can stabilize aggregate outcomes in theory, doing so in practice remains difficult. Many factors influence business cycles— fluctuations in economic activity or booms followed by busts. It is quite difficult for central bankers to gather and correctly interpret data on the state of the business cycle, much less to learn what economic entities are thinking or doing in real time.

Moreover, it is not clear central bankers can account for these decisions and implement monetary policy quickly enough. The size and timing of the effects of changes in monetary policy vary considerably. That is, it might take weeks or months for a bank to decide to lend, and it might take weeks or months for people to borrow funds to spend. Even if central bankers correctly anticipate a future recession, they might not be able to act quickly or forcibly enough to stabilize output.

Diagnosing the sources of recessions might help us understand their effects. Note that the more people want additional goods—following periods of additional wealth, lower interest rates, additional government spending, and a lower interest rate relative to another country—the more aggregate output will rise along with higher prices. Thus, if a recession happens because of changes in these factors we expect to see falling output and a corresponding fall in prices. Alternatively, the more people and firms are willing to produce more goods—following periods of higher expectations of inflation and lower costs of production—the more aggregate output will rise, and the current price level will fall. Thus, if a recession happens because of these factors, we expect to see falling output and a corresponding rise in prices.

Even this word of caution seems unlikely to do much good. That is, the Federal Reserve tries to stabilize economic activity—with those factors of consumption and investment in mind—but it might be a source of instability. To see this, note the relationship between output and inflation during a recession. During most recessions, we observe falling output and falling inflation rates, which suggests people lower their consumption and investment and/or that governments are cutting back on spending. Government spending, however, has been trending upward for most of the last century. This leads us to the following observation: either people change their preferences regarding consumption and investment during recessions or central bank-led changes in real interest rates influence their decisions. Figure 17.1 shows how the three-month treasury rate changes prior to and during recessions.

It seems that most of the recessions in Figure 17.1 follow relatively sudden, substantial increases in interest rates—as measured by the

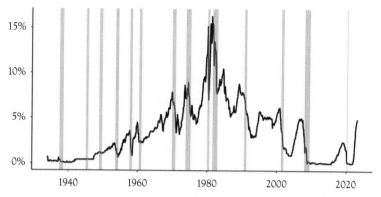

Figure 17.1 Three-month treasury yields, 1934 to 2023

Source: FRED database using fredr.

three-month treasury yield. This does not mean that interest rate hikes or contractionary Federal Reserve monetary policy cause recessions—notice that periods of *growth* also follow relatively sudden, substantial interest rate hikes, for example, in the early 1990s. It does suggest, however, that monetary policy can be implicated as a partial cause of recessions. Such evidence does not bode well for central bankers who want to maintain discretion or to actively use the tools of monetary policy in response to perceived problems with commercial activity.

A Lingering Problem

Even if central bankers know about the factors discussed—and they know stabilization policy is hazardous—they face an additional constraint. Monetary policy via short-term nominal and real interest rates primarily influences people's consumption and investment decisions. Monetary policy becomes a more obtuse policy in response to real shocks or when it comes to changes in production costs many firms face, for example, an unexpected rise in oil prices. Prices will remain elevated after a negative oil shock for as long as it takes for firms to adjust; however, EMP will not alter those conditions, but it will spur people to consume and invest. Such a policy might increase output, but it comes with a rate of inflation higher than that caused by the negative shock alone. To wit, central bankers cannot simultaneously stabilize output and inflation. If central bankers want to maintain a similar amount of output (in response to a negative supply shock), expansionary monetary policy will lead to a higher rate of inflation. If central bankers want to maintain a similar rate of inflation (in response to a negative supply shock), monetary policy will lead to larger reductions in aggregate output.

Competition Is Ever-Present

Financial markets, instruments, and technologies continue to evolve, especially in competitive markets where individuals face incentives to provide valuable products and people seek higher expected returns, additional liquidity, and lower risk. Cryptocurrencies and Non-fungible Tokens (NFTs) are *en vogue*, but no one knows how those assets—if they are assets—will fare in 10 years in competition with other assets. Competition suggests an ongoing process that improves well-being. This conclusion is especially relevant when people act within economic and political institutions that encourage mutually beneficial exchanges. Consistent with the logic Adam Smith spelled out centuries ago, systems of cooperation encourage people to divide labor—and knowledge and capital—which increases productivity and wealth accumulation.

As competition continues throughout financial markets, however, governments will likely continue to regulate the financial system and conduct monetary policy to influence financial intermediaries, the deposit creation process, and the speed and magnitude of various monetary policy channels. The larger point is that our financial system and supporting institutions—the formal and informal rules that influence transactions, lending, and investment—influence our behavior in particular ways. The more our financial system and institutions encourage competition and innovation, the more improvements in well-being will occur. The more our financial system and institutions encourage the pursuit of private over public interests, there will be fewer improvements in well-being.

The institutional setting of central banking, for example, legitimizes intervention in financial markets, lender of last-resort activities, and other attempts to stabilize economic activity. As the rules and details of central banking provide clear expectations about how central bankers are going to behave, the more people can plan. Given the precarious state of central bank independence, however, the detailed ways in which central banking is conducted creates perverse incentives that can serve special interests at the expense of the general welfare.

Monetary Policy as a Guide, Not a Corrective

If students, scholars, and policy makers are interested in improving well-being and in fostering economic development, they should pay more attention to financial markets and the conditions under which those markets allow people to pursue their objectives, for example, to save, borrow, invest, and manage risk, and so on. Governments help in this process by enforcing rules and property rights—to protect life, liberty, and property. As people improve their property rights institutions, they feel more secure in their commercial activity and begin to devise more complex financial operations. Financial systems then serve as an intermediary, generally, between borrowers and lenders; as such, this system connects entrepreneurs and their innovations with people willing to finance such activities. The more a country facilitates and protects such interactions, the more people in those areas will be able to follow their passions and creativity, the more they will serve the interests of others, and the more people can use financial systems to resolve the problems related to transaction costs, risk, and information asymmetry.

To that end, monetary policy can be a useful tool if it guides individuals toward voluntary, mutually beneficial exchange. The more a central bank engages in discretion and/or responds to political pressure, however, the more a central bank becomes a source of rent seeking and instability. The overall debate as to whether a central bank should maintain discretion becomes more pressing as we realize there are additional transmission mechanisms or channels through which monetary policy can be pursued. Having a plethora of channels can be useful, especially when some of them are ineffective or are inappropriate means to provide credit. As banks become a smaller source of credit or when information asymmetry problems become severe, for example, central banks might want to move away from influencing bank balance sheets.

Some of these channels refer to previously explored links between monetary policy and output. Imagine, for instance, that a central bank makes a series of open market purchases, which lowers interest rates and encourages people to buy stocks. People who had previously owned those stocks are now wealthier, from which they might consume more, which ultimately influences output. Alternatively, imagine how expansionary monetary policy lowers interest rates, which encourages people to borrow and ultimately increases the deposit creation process. As banks are better able to resolve information asymmetry problems, this policy enhances banks and the overall financial system. There are other transmission mechanisms, and together, they indicate additional channels through which monetary policy can influence individuals and economic activity for the better. At the same time, they suggest greater caution is in order when a central bank moves to expand the money supply. Such policies can be poorly timed, ill-informed, and can do more harm than good, which is especially true if such interventions erode central bank independence (Mishkin 2009, 70–71).

Conducting monetary policy isn't easy; there are many answers to what central banks should do, and there will always be calls to use monetary policy to *do something*. For example, central banks are often called upon to limit the damages of financial crises and panics, to pop perceived bubbles, and to respond to environmental disasters, wars, and pandemics. The question is not whether central banks can respond to such crises. As we have pointed out throughout the chapters on central banking and monetary policy, central bankers have many tools that can be used to influence individuals and economic activity. The monetary response to COVID-19, for example, hundreds of billions in quantitative easing, helped to keep people fed, housed, and healthy during government-imposed lockdowns and a time of distress. Such measures, however, spurred an historic rise in inflation and an increase in the balance sheet of the Federal Reserve that dwarfed the response to the Financial Crisis of 2007 to 2009.

Central bankers clearly have many tools to respond to crises. However, responding to each crisis might lead to outcomes that run counter to the primary mission of a central bank, that is, long-run financial system stability. What are central bankers to do? Must future crises be met with larger expansionary policies? How far should central banks blur the line between monetary and fiscal policy? At what point do we set aside the centuries-old goals of central banking in favor of being more responsive to pressing issues of the day?

Ultimately, these are normative questions, and tradeoffs abound. We don't have answers to these questions, as they depend on individual values. Economists focus on what will tend to happen, given the rules and incentives people face. Some people might prefer a world in which the central bank is responsive to every crisis, and they are welcome to advance the tools of monetary policy accordingly. At the same time, however, such policies lead to a higher rate of inflation, an increasingly fragile financial system, and lower rates of economic growth. Other people might prefer a world where rules are defined and enforced, and where people have clear expectations about inflation and financial rules, which facilitates economic activity. They are welcome to advance monetary policy to pursue those goals too, but note that it might come at the expense of not cushioning the blow of subsequent crises.

In any event, you now have a working knowledge of money, financial markets, and monetary policy—and how the economic way of thinking illuminates these topics—so you can ponder and answer these questions for yourself.

References

Akerlof, G.A. 1970. "The Market for "Lemons": Quality Uncertainty and the Market Mechanism." *The Quarterly Journal of Economics* 84, no. 3, pp. 488–500. https://doi.org/10.2307/1879431.

Alesina, A. and L.H. Summers. 1993. "Central Bank Independence and Macroeconomic Performance: Some Comparative Evidence." *Journal of Money, Credit and Banking* 25, no. 2, pp. 151–162. https://doi.org/10.2307/2077833.

Almansur, A.M., W.L. Megginson, and L.V. Pugachev. 2020. "Vertical Integration as an Input Price Hedge: The Case of Delta Air Lines and Trainer Refinery." *Financial Management* 49, no. 1, pp. 179–206. https://doi.org/10.1111/fima.12260.

Berg, C., S. Davidson, and J. Potts. 2020. *Understanding the Blockchain Economy: An Introduction to Institutional Cryptoeconomics.* Edward Elgar Pub.

Boettke, P.J., A.W. Salter, and D.J. Smith. 2021. *Money and the Rule of Law: Generality and Predictability in Monetary Institutions.* Cambridge: Cambridge University Press. https://doi.org/10.1017/9781108806787.

Burns, S. 2018. "M-Pesa and the 'Market-Led' Approach to Financial Inclusion." *Economic Affairs* 38, no. 3, pp. 406–421. https://doi.org/10.1111/ecaf.12321.

Collins, C. and G.G. Alvarez. 2015. *Prison Ramen: Recipes and Stories From Behind Bars.* Workman Publishing.

Cowles, A. 1933. "Can Stock Market Forecasters Forecast?" *Econometrica* 1, no. 3, pp. 309–324. https://doi.org/10.2307/1907042.

Cutsinger, B., J. Ingber, and L. Rouanet. August 2020. "Assignats or Death: Inflationary Finance in Revolutionary France." *SSRN Electronic Journal.* https://doi.org/10.2139/ssrn.3674658.

Dincer, N.N. and B. Eichengreen. 2014. "Central Bank Transparency and Independence: Updates and New Measures." *International Journal of Central Banking* 10, no. 1, pp. 189–253.

Durkin, T.A., G. Elliehausen, M.E. Staten, and T.J. Zywicki. 2014. *Consumer Credit and the American Economy,* Illustrated ed. New York, NY: Oxford University Press.

Finer, D.A. 2018. "What Insights Do Taxi Rides Offer Into Federal Reserve Leakage?" Rochester, NY: Social Science Research Network. https://doi.org/10.2139/ssrn.3134953.

"First Nat'l Bank in Plant City v. Dickinson, 396 U.S. 122 (1969)." n.d. https://supreme.justia.com/cases/federal/us/396/122/ (accessed December 22, 2021).

Goetzmann, W.N. 2017. *Money Changes Everything: How Finance Made Civilization Possible*, Revised ed. Princeton, New Jersey Oxford: Princeton University Press.

Greif, A. 1989. "Reputation and Coalitions in Medieval Trade: Evidence on the Maghribi Traders." *The Journal of Economic History* 49, no. 4, pp. 857–882. https://www.jstor.org/stable/2122741.

Gwartney, J., R. Lawson, J. Hall, and R. Murphy. 2021. "Economic Freedom of the World: 2021 Annual Report." Fraser Institute.

Hanke, S. 2021. "Hanke's Inflation Dashboard: Official Statistics Misrepresent Real Inflation Rates." *National Review*. www.nationalreview.com/2021/01/hankes-inflation-dashboard-venezuelas-unwanted-win-argentinas-curious-numbers-sow-confusion/.

Hanke, S. and C. Bushnell. 2017. "On Measuring Hyperinflation: Venezuela's Episode." *World Economics* 18, no. 3, pp. 1–18.

Hansell, S. September 1994. "Gibson Files Lawsuit Over Derivatives." *The New York Times*. www.nytimes.com/1994/09/13/business/gibson-files-lawsuit-over-derivatives.html.

Hayek, F.A. 1945. "The Use of Knowledge in Society." *The American Economic Review* 35, no. 4, pp. 519–530. https://www.jstor.org/stable/1809376.

Hazlett, P.K. and W.J. Luther. August 2020. "Is Bitcoin Money? And What That Means." *The Quarterly Review of Economics and Finance* 77, pp. 144–149. https://doi.org/10.1016/j.qref.2019.10.003.

"Independent Bankers Ass'n v. Marine Midland Bank, 583 F. Supp. 1042 (W.D.N.Y. 1984)." n.d. https://law.justia.com/cases/federal/district-courts/FSupp/583/1042/1598386/ (accessed December 22, 2021).

Johnson, D.B. 1991. *Public Choice: An Introduction to the New Political Economy*, 0 ed. Mountain View, California: Mayfield Pub Co.

Kim, J. 2011. "How Modern Banking Originated: The London Goldsmith-Bankers' Institutionalisation of Trust." *Business History* 53, no. 6, pp. 939–959. https://ideas.repec.org/a/taf/bushst/v53y2011i6p939-959.html.

Logan, T.D. 2017. *Economics, Sexuality, and Male Sex Work*. New York, NY: Cambridge University Press.

Malkiel, B.G. 2019. *A Random Walk Down Wall Street: The Time-Tested Strategy for Successful Investing*, Twelfth ed. New York, NY: W. W. Norton & Company.

Maloney, M.T. and J.H. Mulherin. 2003. "The Complexity of Price Discovery in an Efficient Market: The Stock Market Reaction to the Challenger Crash." *Journal of Corporate Finance, Market Microstructure and Corporate Finance* 9, no. 4, pp. 453–479. https://doi.org/10.1016/S0929-1199(02)00055-X.

McClure, J.E. and D.C. Thomas. 2017. "Explaining the Timing of Tulipmania's Boom and Bust: Historical Context, Sequestered Capital and Market Signals." *Financial History Review* 24, no. 2, pp. 121–141. https://doi.org/10.1017/S0968565017000154.

Meltzer, A.H. 2004. *A History of the Federal Reserve, Volume 1: 1913–1951.* Chicago: University of Chicago Press.

Menger, C. 2007. *Principles of Economics.* Ludwig von Mises Institute. (Originally Published on 1871). www.amazon.com/Principles-Economics-Carl-Menger/dp/1610162021/ref=tmm_pap_swatch_0?_encoding=UTF8&qid=&sr=.

Mises, L.V. 1922. *Socialism: An Economic and Sociological Analysis.* New Haven: Yale University Press.

Mishkin, F.S. 2009. *Monetary Policy Strategy.* Cambridge: Mass; London: The MIT Press.

Mueller, D.C. 2003. *Public Choice III*, 3rd ed. Cambridge University Press.

Munger, M.C. 2018. *Tomorrow 3.0: Transaction Costs and the Sharing Economy.* New York, NY: Cambridge University Press.

Nugent, C. October 2018. "How Hunger Fuels Crime and Violence in Venezuela." *Time.* https://time.com/longform/hunger-crime-violence-venezuela/.

Peltzman, S. 1993. "How George Stigler Changed the Analysis of Regulation." *The University of Chicago Booth School of Business.* www.chicagobooth.edu/review/how-george-stigler-changed-analysis-regulation.

Radford, R.A. 1945. "The Economic Organisation of a P.O.W. Camp." *Economica* 12, no. 48, pp. 189–201. https://doi.org/10.2307/2550133.

Sargent, T.J. and F.R. Velde. 1995. "Macroeconomic Features of the French Revolution." *Journal of Political Economy* 103, no. 3, pp. 474–518. http://www.jstor.org/stable/2138696.

Schrager, A. 2019. *An Economist Walks Into a Brothel: And Other Unexpected Places to Understand Risk.* Portfolio.

Selgin, G.A. 1988. *The Theory of Free Banking*, UK ed. Rowman & Littlefield Publishers.

Sing, B. May 1986. "Possible Damage to Soviet Crops Sends U.S. Commodity Prices Soaring." *Los Angeles Times.* www.latimes.com/archives/la-xpm-1986-05-01-mn-2616-story.html.

Skwire, S. 2014. "The Exchange Value of a Magic Bean Sarah Skwire." https://fee.org/articles/the-exchange-value-of-a-magic-bean/.

Smith, B.D., A.J. Rolnick, and W.E. Weber. 2000. "The Suffolk Bank and the Panic of 1837." *Quarterly Review* 24, no. 2, pp. 3–13. www.minneapolisfed.org:443/research/quarterly-review/the-suffolk-bank-and-the-panic-of-1837.

Smith, S.V. and D. Rafieyan. November 2018. "All Aboard the Bankmobile!" *NPR.* www.npr.org/sections/money/2018/11/08/665897380/all-aboard-the-bankmobile.

Stigler, G.J. 1971. "The Theory of Economic Regulation." *The Bell Journal of Economics and Management Science* 2, no. 1, pp. 3–21. https://doi.org/10.2307/3003160.

Stulz, R.M. 2004. "Should We Fear Derivatives?" *Journal of Economic Perspectives* 18, no. 3, pp. 173–192. https://doi.org/10.1257/0895330042162359.

Traflet, J.M. and R.E. Wright. 2022. *Fearless: Wilma Soss and America's Forgotten Investor Movement.* New York, NY: All Seasons Press.

White, L.H. 1996. *Free Banking in Britain,* 2nd UK ed. Londres: Institute of Economic Affairs.

Wood, J.H. 2008. *A History of Central Banking in Great Britain and the United States,* 1st ed. Cambridge: Cambridge University Press.

Wright, R.E. 2002a. *The Wealth of Nations Rediscovered: Integration and Expansion in American Financial Markets, 1780–1850.* Cambridge: Cambridge University Press. https://doi.org/10.1017/CBO9780511550010.

Wright, R.E. 2002b. "Reforming the US IPO Market: Lessons from History and Theory." *Accounting, Business & Financial History* 12, no. 3, pp. 419–437. https://doi.org/10.1080/09585200210164584.

Wright, R.E. 2005. *The First Wall Street: Chestnut Street, Philadelphia, and the Birth of American Finance.* Chicago, IL: University of Chicago Press. https://press.uchicago.edu/ucp/books/book/chicago/F/bo3634925.html.

Wright, R.E. ed. 2010. *Bailouts: Public Money, Private Profit.* Columbia University Press.

Wright, R.E. 2019a. *Financial Exclusion: How Competition Can Fix a Broken System.* Great Barrington: American Institute for Economics Research.

Wright, R.E. 2019b. "Banking with the Amish—AIER." www.aier.org/article/banking-with-the-amish/ (accessed December 2, 2021).

Wright, R.E. and R. Sylla. 2015. *Genealogy of American Finance.* Columbia Business School Publishing.

About the Authors

Byron B. Carson is an Assistant Professor of Economics and Business at Hampden-Sydney College in Hampden Sydney, Virginia. He regularly teaches courses on introductory economics, money and banking, urban economics, and health economics. He earned his PhD in Economics from George Mason University in 2017, where he was a Graduate Fellow in the F. A. Hayek Program for Advanced Study in Philosophy, Politics, and Economics, and Mercatus Center Dissertation Fellow with the Mercatus Center. He earned his BA in Economics from Rhodes College. His research interests include economic epidemiology, public choice, and Austrian economics. His research has been published in academic journals like *Essays in Economic and Business History*, *The Independent Review*, *The Journal of Private Enterprise*, and *Vaccine*.

Robert E. Wright, PhD from SUNY Buffalo, is the author of 24 books, the editor of five others, and the author of four score-referred journal articles and book chapters. He has taught money and banking at the University of Virginia and money and power at NYU's Stern School of Business. He currently serves the American Institute for Economic Research as a Senior Faculty Fellow.

Index

Made in the USA
Columbia, SC
15 January 2025

51706116R10124